"Who Is Sylvia?"
and Other Stories

"Who Is Sylvia?" and Other Stories

Case Studies in Psychotherapy

Dorothy E. Peven
and
Bernard H. Shulman

Brunner-Routledge
New York and London

Published in 2002 by
Brunner-Routledge
29 West 35th Street
New York, NY 10001

Published in Great Britain by
Brunner-Routledge
27 Church Road
Hove East Sussex
BN3 2FA
United Kingdom

Brunner-Routledge is an imprint of the Taylor & Francis Group.

Printed in the United States of America on acid-free paper.

Design and typography: Jack Donner

10 9 8 7 6 5 4 3 2 1

Library of Congress Cataloging-in-Publication Data is available from the Library of Congress.

ISBN 1–58391–069–7 (pbk)
ISBN 0–415–93434–6 (hbk)

This book is dedicated to our children,
Michael D. Peven, Daniel A. Peven, Charles M. Peven,
Mark M. Shulman, Robert B. Shulman,
and Cynthia Shulman Cassidy

Contents

Introduction

This is a book about a psychodynamic theory and how it is used to understand people and perform psychotherapy. In this book we use a psychological theory that guides our understanding of human behavior and our approach to psychotherapeutics. We believe that human beings are best seen as active organized systems with specific needs and goals, operating within a larger social system, behaving in purposeful ways, sometimes fully conscious of motives, often not, but almost always capable of functioning within a social ecosystem. Many of the theoretical issues presented herein were first suggested by Alfred Adler (1867–1937). Adler's theory is at once a model of human personality, a theory of psychopathology, and the foundation of a treatment method (Peven, 1980).

There are certain basic laws that govern the behavior of human beings, and there are underlying processes that are constant over time. In the past, scientists and philosophers have swung back and forth emphasizing either nature or nurture. But we understand human behavior to be based on biological, social, and psychological factors that interact with each other. Thus, changes in behavior can be influenced by either biological, social, or psychological means.

Sometimes people struggle with unhappy life situations or have repeated problems in their relationships with others. Some carry psychological wounds from past events or have formed mistaken notions about how to cope with the challenges of living in the world. People who are suffering from emotional and psychological problems may need to reexamine themselves in order to understand their own motives and beliefs . . . to comprehend what makes them feel and behave the way they do so that they may make the changes necessary to smooth the business of living. For such people analytic psychotherapy presents an opportunity to refashion their lives.

Analytic psychotherapy is a process by which therapist and client explore the client's problems, behavior, feelings, and thoughts; the client's background and life experiences; the beliefs the client holds within; and the defenses the client uses to avoid "threats" and unpleasantness. We try to understand how all these have led to any current problems, as well as what changes are needed and how to make them.

The cases in this book are about some interesting human beings we have met who became our clients. As we tell their stories we hope to inform the reader about our approach to psychotherapy. We will show how rapport is established, how relationships are maintained, and how we encourage people to know themselves. We also hope to show what we are thinking and how we handle our own feelings during therapeutic sessions.

We chose our cases because they seemed to illuminate our theoretical constructs concerning the psychological nature of human behavior. These cases also demonstrate how we respond to the uniqueness of each individual. Often, we find we must look within ourselves to discern what we are thinking and feeling in order to comprehend the client. We want to help the reader grasp what goes into the analysis of a client and how to proceed once the therapist understands what is required. Our explanations of the psychodynamics of a case will present our point of view, as will our approach to specific treatment goals and treatment methods.

The reader may find the presentation of cases in this book somewhat uneven. We started out by trying to present each case according to a formal structure: (1) Presentation, (2) Psychodynamics, (3) Psychotherapy. However, the people about whom we wrote were alive and real to us and we felt we could tell their stories better if we did not insist on putting the story into a formal case presentation. During the process of psychotherapy the client's narrative unfolds; it becomes more elaborate and more sharply defined. As the therapy proceeds, we are continuously refining our understanding of the client. Rather than put all of the stories into the same format, it became clear that each story begged to be told in its own way. And while this is a book about psychotherapy, it is basically a book of stories.

The first chapters in the book are about theory and therapy. Our approach to theory and therapy is informed by Alfred Adler's Individual Psychology with its emphasis on the uniqueness of the individual and the individual's relationship to society. Starting with chapter 3, we will present cases in which the formal diagnosis of the client falls into one of the categories listed in the *Diagnostic and Statistical Manual of the American Psychiatric Association*, (APA, 1994; hereafter, DSM-IV).

The DSM-IV is a tool for categorizing and statistical measurement. As such, it performs a valuable service. However, the DSM-IV does not explain the psychodynamics nor the psychogenesis of each disorder. As we tell the story of each of our cases, we will go behind the descriptive categories to discuss those issues not addressed by the DSM-IV: early life experiences, family settings, learned behaviors, and the construction of values and choice of goals. We will show the tools we use to discover and identify the scripts individuals fashion for their lives and how "symptoms" can often be self-selected modes of behavior.

This book describes people with problems who sought psychotherapy. Sometimes we were quite helpful to them, other times, less so. Some people learned a great deal and made significant changes. Others could not bring themselves to do what was necessary. And sometimes, although no great change took place, the therapeutic experience was most satisfying to both parties.

References

American Psychiatric Association. (1994). *Diagnostic and statistical manual of mental disorders* (4th ed.). Washington, DC: Author.

Peven, D. E. (1980). Adlerian psychotherapy. In R. Herink (Ed.), *The psychotherapy handbook*. New York: New American Library.

1

Psychodynamic Theory

The theory presented by Alfred Adler and elaborated by his followers views human beings as members of a social species who live in social groups and are socialized to be "human." According to this theory, human behavior is best understood in a social setting. It is, in fact, through the establishment and maintenance of human relationships that people give meaning to their lives.

The early social scientists tended to seek the "cause" of social behavior in either biological, environmental, or economic factors. While Karl Marx (1818–1883) and William Sumner (1840–1910) attributed all human behavior to the influence of cultural institutions. Adler and others understood human behavior could not be explained in simplistic, mechanical terms. For example, Kurt Lewin (1890–1947) suggested in his Field Theory that:

> The world, as experienced by the individual at a given point in time, is his life space, which always includes both the person and his psychological environment. . . . Behavior is always a function of this life space, which in turn, is always a product of the interaction between the person and his environment. . . . (Lewin, in Schellenberg, 1978, p. 70)

Horton Cooley (1865–1929) and George Herbert Mead (1863–1931) were among the early social theorists who considered that personality and behavior could only be understood as a product of the interaction between social demands and individual needs. They believed that behavior is subjectively determined within a specific social context and described the social field in which Adler's concept of the "Life-Style" could develop.

> [It is] not heredity and not environment that are [the] determining factors [in determining personality]. Both are giving only the frame and the influences which are answered by the individual in regard to his styled creative power. (Adler, in Ansbacher & Ansbacher, 1956, intro.)

Recent studies in cognitive theory by social constructivists suggest that theorists are once again paying attention to the position of the early social scientists and find that they are, in essence, in agreement with them (Beck, 1976; Freeman & Urschel, 1997; Jones, 1995; Mahoney et al., 2001).

Inferiority Feelings and Compensation: The Self-Appraisal

We are born without fully developed faculties and are, therefore, dependent for a long period of time. As a consequence, we bond with our caretakers, mother in particular. This bonding to another is what makes us human and from this initial bond comes the preparation for socialization. During the course of socialization we begin to find our place in the social group. In fact, our sense of self is associated with the perception of self within the group setting. This establishes identity, the sense of who one is in relation to others (Master, 1991). As formulated by Mead, Cooley, and Adler, self-conception is considered a function of our sense of personal worth and adequacy and our evaluation of the attitudes of others toward us.

The early experiences of childhood have an important effect on future conduct; they provide the early templates for our behavior and give us the material we use to build personality and character. Children require parenting that fosters a sense of security, courage, and prosocial conduct. Failing that, the opportunities for the child to feel inferior, incapable, or inadequate are increased. If a child is pampered, neglected, or rejected there is a strong possibility that the child will not develop the self-confidence and courage required to meet the developmental challenges.

The child that is pampered has less chance to learn persistence in the face of difficulty, and the rejected child often develops loss of self-esteem and trust. Childhood experiences such as abuse, abandonment, loss of security and conversely, overprotection and overindulgence, interfere with the development of internal aspects of personality (values, self-appraisal) that promote a smoother development to healthy and constructive mental attitudes in adulthood.

Feeling inadequate to meet life's challenges (the "feeling of inferiority"), the child tries to compensate for assumed deficiencies—the resulting behavior can be either prosocial or antisocial, useful or useless.

The desire for power, achievement, uniqueness, and so forth can be demonstrated throughout history, across cultures, and over time. The desire for mastery and competent coping can be seen readily in most children and it is common for children to compare their skills and rate themselves against each other. But the actual differences in skill do not necessarily lead to inferiority feelings. Such feelings have to do with perceptions of social status. This feeling can also be understood as "low self-esteem."

Attempts to preserve self-esteem or enhance it are called *compensations*. Compensations can be normative and socially acceptable or deviant and unacceptable. Some compensations are defensive, such as withdrawal and avoidance of challenging situations. Other compensations are offensive, such as seeking out obstacles to overcome or finding new ways to deal with challenges.

Arnold Rose (a Symbolic Interaction theorist) suggests that all neurosis can be understood as arising from a negative evaluation of the self: "[The] 'self,' reflecting the reactions of others toward it, is an important intervening variable in human conduct..." (Rose, 1962, p. 540).

Theodor Litman writes: "Self-conception is a function of the individual's sense of personal worth and adequacy and an evaluation of the attitudes of others toward him" (Litman, in Rose, 1962, p. 559). The more current literature on the "self" leans towards a view of the self as a

> kind of modern, atomistic self [which] aspires to an extreme sort of individual autonomy, separateness, and self-definition and confronts a natural and social world to which it has no essential ties . . . this notion of the self . . . enshrines the modern ideal of "freedom as self-autonomy" and thus reflects the intense . . . anti-authoritarian temper of the modern era. (Manaster, et al. 1999. p. 477)

Although we use the word "self" in many different ways in everyday speech and in this book, our concept of self is inclined toward the Individual Psychologist's viewpoint. In contrast to the "modern" concept of self as an autonomous self-contained unit,

> [i]n the Adlerian view, individual purpose and fulfillment go hand in hand with deepening social interest, with a growing sense of belonging to wider communities and traditions, and with being of service to them. Thus, Individual Psychology is in a unique position to explain why high levels of self-esteem, which usually appear to reflect a modern, highly individualistic sense of personal dignity or worth, are so often correlated with . . . self-defeating strategies in living. (Manaster et al., 1999, p. 478)

Striving for Significance: Movement in the Psychic Life

We understand each human being as an organism traveling through time and space to meet a destiny. This destiny is imagined by the individual as an ideal state of being. Since the organism is always moving as if there is an end point (or final goal) it is possible to examine behavior from the point of view of the direction of the movement. This striving of the organism is always understood within a social context; that is, toward, away, or against people in the social field (Horney, 1945).

The direction of movement is influenced by this dominant goal that is selected according to the individual's unique perception of the ideal state—bliss, paradise, nirvana. The underlying direction of movement is often largely unconscious. The dynamic aspects of personality—interests, impulses, tropisms, drives—are all part of the unifying system, which is always in movement. The unification is achieved by the existence of a goal that creates the direction of movement for the system. The movement toward a "fictional" goal is continuous, it is constant, and it is maintained throughout life (Lombardi, et al., 1996).

The Unconscious

For Sigmund Freud, the unconscious was a storehouse of instinctual drives and impulses kept in check by a censoring, repressing ego. Our position is different. We do not believe that the unconscious is always inimical, a wild beast that needs to be tamed. Most of us are not always aware of what we are doing, nor do we always understand or want to acknowledge why we do what we do. We tend to protect our self-esteem by denying, rationalizing, blaming others, and using other self-protective forms of thinking. We want to shield ourselves from shame, guilt, and fear; from having to face things we do not want to face.

People are only dimly aware of the constructs that underlie their innermost motives, their biased perceptions, their idiosyncratic, highly subjective views of the world and people. These views, formed in early childhood, are private, somewhat autistic, often nonconsensual, and are never fully explicated and examined until psychotherapy. They form a "private logic" for understanding the world and acting in it.

In addition to these unapprehended constructs, our biases tend to create selectivity in our perceptions so that we filter out information that would require us to change our biased beliefs.

In this way we reinforce our private pictures of reality. We are usually not aware of how we are being influenced by our private logic, by pictures of the world that are no longer true, by decisions made long ago for reasons that are no longer recalled.

Finally, it is not economical to be fully conscious of all of our activities, for it would be a hindrance if we had to give every bit of incoming information equal weight. We are eased through life because we perceive selectively and prioritize.

The Emotions

Emotions are energizers of behavior—dynamic forces that produce movement. Thought alone does not lead to action, but thoughts and emotions tend to concur and effect each other. Emotional arousal can be produced by a sequence of thoughts as well as vice versa. For example, if depressed, we have depressive thoughts. On the other hand, emotions can be evoked by cognitive appraisals; e.g., "That girl is thinner than I am and prettier too. I'll never be that pretty and thin. I am a failure."

In time, we learn to call forth our emotions in order to carry out an intention, to accomplish a purpose. Thus, we summon anger in order to intimidate another, to display bravery, or to win an argument by "overpowering" another.

Although we are born with certain built-in emotional responses, we learn to use emotions as strategies in the pursuit of our private goals. The idea that passions can be overwhelming is not accepted as an excuse for inappropriate behavior. In ordinary life situations people are responsible for their own emotions.

Others, such as the French existentialist Jean-Paul Sartre, have also seen the emotions as "strategies for coping with a difficult world. [Emotions] are, accordingly, our responsibility, not mere excuses." Sartre argues that emotions have "'intentionality,' 'finality' or purpose. A person is not caused to be angry, fall in love, grow resentful. He or she has reasons for doing so. . . . Emotions are our own doing. . . . [They are] strategies, knowingly and willfully under-taken" (Solomon, 1996, p. 11).

The Life-Style

We have previously said the individual's striving towards the goal of significance and social belonging could be observed as a pattern that manifests itself early in life and plays like a musical theme throughout each lifetime. This theme, which Adler called the "Life-Style," functions as a blueprint for action, but remains primarily unconscious; that is, outside awareness. This life-style is both a perceptual and a coping style and thus is demonstrated in all aspects of a person's behavior.

The life-style pattern is formed and developed early in life when experience is limited and cognitive abilities are still under-developed. Observations and interpretations about social living and the behavior of others are made before language develops, before symbolization matures. Interpersonal transactions and the behavior of others in the environs influence these interpretations. But without the full ability to discriminate and to evaluate impressions, people come to mistaken conclusions and assumptions about what it takes to meet the challenges of living in a world of others. Wilson quotes Francis Bacon: "[T]he mind, hastily and without choice, imbibes and treasures up the first notice of things, from whence all the rest proceed, errors must forever prevail, and remain uncorrected" (Bacon, in Wilson, 1998, p. 23).

As children we affect, by our behavior and interactions, the forces around us. As adults we construe, we think, and we draw conclusions about what is happening around us and make decisions based on the mistaken apperceptions we formed as children, unaware that we are using fictional constructs based upon long past experiences from which we have drawn biased conclusions.

The Creative Self

Intervening between the stimuli acting upon us and the response we make to stimuli are our biased apperceptions. It is these biases that determine how we respond. Influenced by our genetic inheritance and the social environment, we make unconscious decisions about appropriate behavior and act accordingly. Through the use of selective perception we extract from the environment whatever information we need to aid us in the expression of our life-styles, and we block out information that could create cognitive dissonance. Adler called this self-organizing principle the "creative self" and believed that it is the "creative self" that determines the idiosyncratic nature of behavior.

> The creative self is the yeast that acts upon the facts of the world and transforms these facts into a personality that is subjective, dynamic, unified, personal, and uniquely stylized. The creative self gives meaning to life; it creates the goal as well as the means to the goal. . . . [It] is the active principle of human life. . . . (Hall & Lindzey, 1970, p. 127)

Behavior is influenced by but not determined by instinct, by genetic inheritance, or by environment, but is more largely determined by learning, making choices, and by choosing between alternatives. We respond to life challenges in an adaptive, creative manner.

> That is, we have formed ourselves and are, therefore responsible for ourselves. [We] cannot blame another, the past, or uncontrollable forces for [our] current condition. (Peven, 1980, p. 10)

Social Interest

In later years Adler, who was an advocate of social justice, enlarged his conception of the "self-actualized" personality to include the concept of social interest or *gemeinschaftsgefuhl*— more literally, "feeling of community." Social Interest is the feeling of having something in common with other people—those who have come before and those who will be in the future. It is demonstrated by cooperation with society, with the feeling of comradeship, and by the willingness to take responsibility for preserving and promoting the welfare of the larger society. In fact, the ability to cooperate can be understood as a measure of the development of social interest.

> The socialization of the individual is not achieved at the cost of repression, but is afforded through an innate human ability, which, however, needs to be developed. It is this ability which Adler called ... social interest. Because the individual is embedded in a social situation, social interest becomes crucial for his adjustment. (Ansbacher & Ansbacher, 1956, p. 2)

The Neurosis: Psychopathology

Pathology is a complex matter with differing "causes" and explanations and can be seen from many points of view. Psychodynamic issues are not always the main source of pathology, and we do not expect psychopathology to always be our main concern.

Certain people are born with constitutional pathology, that is, there is something wrong with the structure of the body (anatomy) or the workings of the body (physiology). Others are subject to disease. Whatever is "wrong" can be the result of genetic factors, anatomical changes, disease, or toxins. Therefore, one of the things we do consider when first meeting a new client is the relationship between constitution and experience and how they interact with each other. We also understand what every mother with more than one child knows—children are born with differing personality traits (Costa & McRae, 2001). Whoever comes into this world with a timid soul is going to be subject to social anxiety and will behave in accordance; that is, that person will display inhibited and social avoidant traits.

The *Diagnostic and Statistical Manual (DSM-IV) of the American Psychiatric Association* identifies clusters of symptoms and gives different clusters different names according to the most prevalent symptom. As previously stated, the DSM-IV is largely a description of certain categories of behavior. It is our opinion that many of the different diagnoses in the DSM-

IV are cross-sectional descriptions of the *behavior of the moment*. Symptoms from different diagnostic categories overlap, but a client's symptoms can (and often do) change. Symptoms will wax and wane depending on the exigencies of life experiences. Thus, clusters of symptoms do not actually describe a particular person in a particular situation.

We understand psychopathology as a pattern of behavior that results from mistaken perceptions. These mistakes are largely unconscious and are associated with threats to the self-esteem, and/or issues such as social status, safety, security, and being in the world (*Dasein*).

Sometimes a headache is only a headache, but sometimes a headache can serve another purpose such as avoiding an unpleasant task. Life continually presents us with difficulties and we are frequently called upon to deal with circumstances that require an increase of effort and courage. We regard psychogenic symptoms as safeguarding tactics used to excuse the individual from some life situation the person is unwilling to face. When a difficult life situation presents itself—illness, death, divorce— we are required to search for solutions. Those who live with an apprehensive attitude meet a challenging situation with the use of avoidance mechanisms such as the development of symptoms. We see certain psychogenic symptoms as *excuses in the service of avoidance* and believe it is logical to escape a perceived danger when frightened.

Thus, neurotic symptoms are power tools, offensive weapons used to affect the outcome of a situation. They defend against the loss of self-esteem and help avoid anticipated failures. But as stated above, symptoms can change and often do when they no longer serve their purpose.

> In the eyes of the Individual Psychologist, the main significance of the symptom lies in its service to the individual. . . . Thus, a symptom is described as the means of securing a triumph, of retiring from danger, of reproaching another, [or] compelling others to concern themselves continuously with [the sick person]. (Shulman & Mosak, 1967, p. 123)

This is an approach to life that requires a certain amount of subterfuge and indirection because life is seen as so difficult. People who feel intimidated by challenges, who feel inadequate to cope without special advantage use such arrangements. We see this symptomatic behavior as a mistaken effort to adapt to the requirements of living—"misguided adaptive arrangements used by discouraged people" (Peven & Shulman, 1986, p. 123). It is just such mistakes that are treated as correctable.

In summary, neurosis is regarded as a frightened retreat from the challenges of life by the use of symptoms. It is the mark of a discouraged person. This discouragement is considered a result of constitutional inadequacy, mistaken apperceptions, of faulty rearing, social rejection, and/or traumatic life experiences that lead to the perception that one is not adequate to cope with life.

References

Ansbacher, H., & Ansbacher, R. (Eds.) (1956). *The individual psychology of Alfred Adler*. New York: Basic Books.

Beck, A. (1976). *Cognitive therapy and the emotional disorders*. New York: International Universities Press.

Costa, P. T., Jr. & McRae R. R. (2001). A theoretical context for adult temperament. In T. D. Wachs & G. A. Kohnstamm (Eds.), *Temperament in context* (pp. 1–21). Mahwah, NJ: Lawrence Erlbaum Associates.

Freeman, A., & Urschel, J. (1997). Individual psychology and cognitive-behavioral therapy: A cognitive therapy perspective. *Journal of cognitive psychotherapy, 11*, 165–180.

Hall, C., & Lindzey, G. (1970). *Theories of personality* (2nd ed.). New York: John Wiley & Sons.

Horney, K. (1945). *Our inner conflicts*. New York: W.W. Norton.

Jones, J. (1995). Constructivism and Individual Psychology: Common ground for dialogue. *Journal of Individual Psychology, 51*, 231–243.

Lombardi, D. N., Melchior, D. J., Murphy J. G., & Brinkerhoff, A. (1996). The ubiquity of the life style. *Journal of Individual Psychology, 32*(1), 31–41.

Manaster, G. J., Weinfeld, M. B., Richardson, F. C., & Mays, M. (1999). The absence of self in Adlerian research. *Journal of Individual Psychology, 55*(4), 474–484.

Master, B. (1991). Constructivism and the creative power of the self. *Journal of Individual Psychology, 47*, 447–455.

Mahoney, M., Freeman, A. & DeVito, P. (Eds.). (In press). *Cognition and Psychotherapy*. New York: Springer Publishing Co.

Peven, D. (1980). Adlerian psychotherapy. In Herink, R. (Ed.). *The psychotherapy handbook*. New York: New American Library.

Peven, D., & Shulman, B. (1986). Adlerian psychotherapy. In I. Kutash & A. Wolf (Eds.), *Psychotherapists' casebook* (pp. 101–123). San Francisco: Jossey-Bass.

Rose, A. M. (Ed.) (1962). *Human behavior and social processes: An interactionist approach*. Boston: Houghton Mifflin Co.

Schellenberg, J. A. (1978). *Masters of social psychology*. New York: Oxford University Press.

Shulman, B. H., & Mosak, H. (1967). Various purposes of symptoms. *Journal of Individual Psychology, 23,* 79–87.

Solomon, R. (1996). *No excuses: Existentialism and the meaning of life* (Part 11). Springfield, VA: The Teaching Company.

Wilson, E. (1998). *Consilience: The unity of knowledge*. New York: Alfred A. Knopf.

2

Psychodynamic Psychotherapy

We understand psychotherapy as an interpersonally oriented learning process during the course of which the therapist and client enter into a collaborative relationship. This relationship permits the exploration of the conscious and unconscious motivations for behavior. And it is the vehicle through which change takes place.

The Therapeutic Relationship

Different psychotherapists work in different ways and different patients need different approaches. We ourselves follow a philosophy that says that change is possible. The therapist's job is to help the client recognize that something needs to be changed and what that something is. People who do not believe there is need for change are not suited for psychotherapy.

Sometimes when clients first come to see us they are too distraught to engage in exploratory behavior and need help to calm their upset emotions. Often, people are so defensive and frightened that they find it difficult to trust us or to admit to any problem. Our job is to reassure and help them to feel more secure with us. Sometimes an acute stressful life situation requires immediate attention. Psychotherapy requires a certain amount of tranquility so that excessive anxiety, depression, and other emotions are quieted and the work can begin. We try to promote and enhance an ambience that permits people to become coworkers sharing the same therapeutic goals in what is called a *therapeutic alliance*. This relationship is crucial for psychotherapy or the necessary work will not get done.

The Role of the Therapist

The therapist is a guide . . . a guide to the client's "inner psyche" and an interpreter of the "outer" world. All therapists bring their habitual manner of relating into the consultation room, just as do their clients. Therefore, it is important for therapists not to allow their own personal biases and prejudices to interfere with the client's treatment.

The psychotherapeutic relationship is a face-to-face encounter requiring good will on the part of the therapist who tries to nurture, who leads and elicits trust from clients. The client who comes for help wants to find in the therapist an expert, a trustworthy friend, and an ally, perhaps a mentor, perhaps a parent figure. If the therapist can supply some of these desired qualities, plus validation, understanding, as well as offering helpful suggestions, the client will engage in the relationship.

Clients often want their therapists to give them the unconditional positive regard that parents give to their children, a demand the therapist cannot fill. Yet the strong interest demonstrated by the therapist has healing power. We believe it is this intense, caring interest that helps clients to continue through all the ups and downs of the course of therapy more than any particular technique (Carlson, 2000, pp. 6–7).

Transference and Countertransferance

Jourard explains the nature of the therapeutic relationship:

> No patient can be expected to drop all his defenses and reveal himself except in the presence of someone who he believes is for him, and not for a theory, dogma or technique. I believe that if the therapist abandons all attempts to shape his patient's behavior according to some prede-

termined scheme, and instead strives to know and
respond honestly to what he has learned, and to establish a relationship of I and Thou, then he is doing his job
as well as it can be done. Therapy proceeds through
honest responses to this very person by this very person.
(Jourard, in Carlson & Slavik, 1997, p. 11.)

Most therapists understand that the therapeutic relationship
itself has a healing effect. It is understood that "warm involve-
ment with the client and communication of a new perspective
can lead to therapeutic change" (Shulman, 1988, p. 95).

Adler believed that transference is the natural tendency of two
human beings engaged in a common task, over a period of time,
to develop a bond to each other, and that the Freudian concept
that a "transference neurosis" had to develop and be "worked
through" may unnecessarily prolong the course of psychotherapy.

People like to talk about themselves, especially when the
listener is interested and nonjudgmental. Many of our clients,
when they start to feel better, can be charming, humorous, and
likable. As they lose inhibitions and relate freely we get to know
the real person and when they become comfortable, there can
be pleasure in their company. We do not consider this "counter-
transference." However, male therapists in particular have to
watch themselves about a tendency to be attracted to good-
looking women. And women therapists tend to be attracted to
or impressed by powerful males. Therapists might be prone to
treat rich or well-known clients differently or to look down on
clients of lower social class. And all therapists must be aware of
personal prejudices that might interfere with their ability to
understand and appreciate the client's experience.

Resistance

Resistance is a certain behavior on the part of the client that
impedes the course of therapy, and it has a quality of opposition
and fearfulness that is different than a lack of understanding.

While it may be a product of the therapist's clumsiness, this is usually not the case. Some people do not feel safe enough to open themselves to the therapist. Others may want to conceal their hostility. Certain clients do not trust and will not expose themselves for fear of being hurt. Putting oneself in the hands of another is very difficult for most people and requires a certain degree of faith in the comradeship of the other.

When the client isn't ready, we wait. When the client is ready, resistance falls away.

The Goals of Psychotherapy

Although this is a brief introduction to the theory and practice of psychodynamic psychotherapy, the broad implications for the goals of psychotherapy become evident. We seek to change mistakes: mistakes about the self and others; mistakes about the situation and its demands; and mistakes about values, meanings, and goals.

We try to help the client develop social interest, "the feeling of caring and belonging and active participation in constructive human endeavor" (Mosak & Shulman, 1974). We see this emphasis on social interest as enlightened self-interest. Helping another and having the other appreciate it is rewarding and allows the giver to feel significant.

> Another goal is to decrease inferiority feelings and overcome discouragement and pessimism. Implicit in both these goals is the goal of changing errors in perception and mistaken unconscious goals into more accurate perceptions and more appropriate goals. A more positive self-image, a more optimistic view of life and its possibilities, a more courageous attitude, and active prosocial behavior are considered desirable results. (Peven & Shulman, 1986, p. 123)

Human beings are social animals who need social relationships; all human beings are in some form of relationship to the others around them. We seek to help others to learn how to be effective in interpersonal relations. We want our clients to be able to meet the tasks of life and to deal with the challenges that life presents so that they are enabled to live comfortably in the world.

Assessment: The Material Examined

Assessment is the process of investigation and continues throughout the course of therapy. As stated above, the distinguishing characteristic of our psychotherapy is *what* is assessed and interpreted.

We seek to assess what really troubles people and why. What are they afraid of? What do they want? How do they see the world and themselves in it? And what is it they feel they can do and can't do? What are their hurts and what are their victories? Who are they?

Family Constellation

One particular way in which we understand the client's view of self, life, and the requirements for living is to assess the client's life-style.

Human beings are complex organisms, incompletely programmed at birth for full functioning. As a result, a large part of our time in childhood is spent in information-seeking so that we can create a program that will help us to function. Mistakes are made. These mistakes and our early childhood experiences influence our perceptions of the "self" and the world. These experiences take place in our family of origin.

The family constellation is a sociogram of early family life and helps us to understand some of the determining factors in the creation of a client's personality. Among the matters examined are sibling relationships, ordinal position,* family values, family atmosphere, and parent-child relationships. The conclusions drawn from the early childhood pageant reflect how the past is

---

*Adlerians were probably the first psychologists to pay attention to birth order.

used to construct a picture of the present. Conversely, the way in which we understand the past is influenced by the way in which we view the present.

Early Recollections

Behavior is contemporaneous, but we use the information from the past to inform us about today's required behavior. Among the many experiences of childhood there are certain memories that leave a strong impression, and it is these memories that become the landmarks of our cognitive map of the world. People use early memories as if they were the documents containing the information required for day-to-day living—the program that is called up in order to make a decision. We do not try to find forgotten (or "repressed") memories, but ask for early recollections (ER) that are remembered. As Helene Papanek writes, "ERs reflect the person's guidelines for his behavior. . . . These old memories are not *reasons* for present behavior [and]. . . they do not *determine* present behavior" (Papanek, in Carlson & Slavik, 1999, p. 82).

In fact, early recollections are used as a *projective* technique.

> The earliest recollections, in common with the dream . . .
> have the advantage of being completely unstructured
> . . . the production is influenced only by the individual's
> perceptual framework which selectively focuses upon the
> particular memories he produces. . . . (Mosak, 1958, p. 61)

The way in which we view the past is influenced by the way in which we view the present and vice versa. Memory is a dynamic process. It changes as mood changes, as perceptions change. Therefore, we are not surprised to find the early recollections change during the course of psychotherapy. An early recollection that was originally designed to remind the person of one point of view may change to represent something different. Early recollections are like illustrations using nonverbal language. They illuminate the client's beliefs and help in understanding the unique language of each client.

Unconscious Material: Dreams

Dreams, expressive movements (body language), slips and errors in language as well as emotional responses and symptomatology are all material for discussion in psychotherapy since they all employ the same dynamisms, that is, they are all psychic phenomena. Therefore, we often ask our clients to write down their dreams and bring them in for discussion.

The Adlerian interpretation of dreams benefits from the insights of Freud and Jung, but offers some unique concepts about the meaning and purpose of dreams. Uniquely in the world of psychology, we understand the dream as purposefully creating an emotional state in the dreamer. Behavior is organized toward a psychic goal, and the emotions are the catalysts of action. Therefore, the purposive nature of the dream is the emotion created, whether the dreamer remembers the dream or not. According to this idea, people have nightmares because they have "some private reason for frightening [themselves]" (Shulman, 1973, p. 64).

The content of the dream tells us about matters of everyday life. We ask for dreams from clients because we understand them to be a rehearsal for the future, a method of problem solving, or an admonition to the self (a reproach). Since dreams use symbolic imagery and language that often reflects unconscious feelings we have an opportunity to learn about the inner world of the client.

Sometimes, the stuff of the unconscious is full of what we are ashamed of, what we don't want to deal with and don't want to admit to ourselves. Some material has been deliberately forgotten because it is painful to remember, and certain unconscious memories are kept in storage files. We try to recover this material, and dreams are one method on the "road to the unconscious."

> [We] . . . ask for dreams from the patient [and] use them to understand and define problem areas, to predict the near future direction of movement of the patient, to help us to understand the patient's characteristic lines of movement (the life style), to alert [ourselves] to the patient's movement in the therapeutic relationship, to

show the patient these aspects of himself, and to teach
the patient to observe and understand his own dynamics.
(Shulman, 1973, p. 71)

We often find that when clients begin to analyze and understand their dreams themselves, they are probably nearing the end
of therapy.

Psychodynamic Analysis

We use the material from the examination of the client's family
constellation and early recollections to construct a set of core
cognitions about the client. The core cognitions involve the self
in the world. One way of constructing this is to fill in the blanks
in the rubric:
   I am.......
   Life is........
   Therefore........

I am:
   Answers questions about the self-concept, a set of convictions expressing the person's feelings about the self that includes
the self-identity ("who am I") and the self-image (an evaluation
of the self), perceived inferiorities, goals, and ambitions.

Life is:
   This is a set of convictions about the world outside of the
subjective self, the world of people. Are people friendly, competitive, hostile? "How do people treat me? Do I have the power to
influence the outcome of significant events?"
   Included are ideas and ideals about the significant issues of
life; e.g., one may value honor above all else, another may value
prestige or money. And still another will make safety and security important. Moral judgments about what *should be* can also
be found here.

Therefore:
   These are judgments about behavior, what to do and how to

do it—the conclusions made from the self-image and the image of the world. "If I am thus and so, and the world is that which, then I must obviously do the following. . . ." People make decisions about what they have to do to make life work for them and the decisions are based on their conceptions of self, life, and people.

The material collected is used to help the therapist understand the psychic world of the client, but the process of investigation continues throughout psychotherapy. New material may surface with the relaxation of defensive maneuvers, making possible a clearer understanding of the client.

Interpretation

Analytic psychotherapy is a process by which therapists and clients examine the clients' problems, behaviors, feelings, and thoughts. The psychotherapy is designed so that it enables clients to explore themselves, to understand their motives, their beliefs, and the meaning they give to their lives. All analytic psychotherapies depend on interpretation as one method to help clients to change. Understanding can lead to change, so we try to help clients recognize that something needs to be changed and what that something is.

Interpretation is made in terms of motives, goals, and movement:

> Most important to the Adlerian therapist is to watch the patient's movement. The direction of movement reveals the goal—to avoid a feared task, to excuse oneself from an onerous task, to keep distance from what is not desired, and to approach what is desired. (Peven & Shulman, 1986, p. 123)

The source material for interpretation is the family constellation, early recollections, longitudinal history, unconscious material, and recurrent behavior patterns in the solution of the life tasks. We explain behavior within the framework of the lifestyle, and emphasize the purpose of the behavior rather than the cause. The intention of interpretation is to enhance insight, i.e., to promote a change in perception so that a new view of reality results.

Interpretation is also made in terms of current behavior. We pay attention to the meaning of symptoms, the course of the therapeutic relationship, and the choices the client is making along with any self-defeating behavior.

> Mistaken perceptions are sympathetically but thoroughly brought into the open for examination. Their sources are identified in the early childhood situation, and current troublesome behaviors are interpreted both as a relic of past learning and as having current safeguarding value. These behaviors defend against loss of self-esteem and help avoid anticipated failures. (Peven & Shulman, 1986, p. 123)

We interpret what people are up to rather than what they say—"real" intentions versus "good" intentions. We interpret nonverbal behavior—posture, gesture, facial expressions. We ask, what strategies are used for coping? And we look at the way a person responds to life's developmental challenges.

When we are able to show people that they've made a mistake and they are able to gain a new perspective, a window of opportunity opens and change is possible. Clients often enjoy a feeling of empowerment that follows a new perspective.

The Process of Psychotherapy

The process of change requires that clients recognize the need for modification and then decide whether or not they *want* to change. When they are willing, clients learn that old behaviors and old beliefs can be replaced with new behaviors and new beliefs. Change endures when it becomes clear that this new outlook makes life easier.

We look for insight on the part of the client, but insight alone does not lead to modifications in behavior. The therapist has to facilitate change, and this is done by promoting hope, encouraging risk, and exposing fictions. We advocate prosocial behaviors and positive self-esteem by validating, teaching, explaining, and coaching.

Finally, we seek to help people find meaning in their lives. Some people find meaning in life through relationships, some through accomplishments. Our point of view is that the most satisfying meanings are found in relationships that are mutually encouraging and mutually beneficial. The conventional morals and ethics provide appropriate guidelines for good human relationships, for the life of the psyche benefits from the warmth and comfort of others.

References

Carlson, J. (2000). Individual psychology in the year 2000 and beyond: Astronaut or dinosaur? Headline or footnote? *Journal of Individual Psychology*, 56(1), 3–13.

Jourard, S. (1997). I-thou relationship versus manipulation in counseling and psychotherapy. In J. Carlson & S. Slavik (Eds.), *Techniques in Adlerian psychology* (pp. 7–12). Washington, DC: Accelerated Development (Taylor & Francis Group).

Mosak, H. (1977). Early recollections as a projective technique. In *On purpose* (pp. 60–75). Chicago: Alfred Adler Institute.

Mosak, H. & Shulman, B. (1974). *Individual psychotherapy 1: A syllabus*. Chicago: Alfred Adler Institute.

Papanek, H. (1999). The use of early recollections in psychotherapy. In J. Carlson & S. Slavick (Eds.), *Techniques in Adlerian psychotherapy* (pp. 81–88). Washington, DC: Accelerated Development (Taylor & Francis Group).

Peven, D., & Shulman, B. (1986). Adlerian psychotherapy. In I. Kutash & A. Wolf (Eds.), *Psychotherapist's casebook* (pp. 101–123). San Francisco: Jossey-Bass.

Shulman, B. (1973). An adlerian theory of dreams. In *Contributions to individual psychology*. (pp.60–80). Chicago: Alfred Adler Institute Publishers.

Shulman, B. (1988). Dissecting the elements of therapeutic change: A response. *Journal of Cognitive Psychotherapy: An International Quarterly*, 2 (2)10–15.

3

The Metamorphosis

As Gregor Samsa awoke one morning . . . he found himself trans-
formed . . . into a gigantic insect.

> —Franz Kafka, "The Metamorphosis" (1915)

The Presentation

George was ugly. He knew he was ugly. His ears were perpendicu-
lar to his head and his chin receded. When he smiled one could see
that his teeth were crooked, but he seldom smiled. He wore thick
glasses and a mournful visage. He came to us complaining that he
suffered from anxiety, depression, and compulsive rituals that he
"couldn't control." He blamed his anxiety on his job, his depression
on his wife, and explained the rituals by saying he was "cheated" as
a child. He did not believe he was responsible in any way for his
unhappy life. Life, nature, and the vagaries of fate were to blame.

He justified his antagonistic attitude: "I was cheated. I was
cheated out of good looks, money, love, and a happy childhood."
In line with this belief he told the story of a lonely, frightened child
and adolescent who spent his early years lying, stealing, and
cheating others, trying to get even.

In fact, as an adult, George continued to steal, but now he did
it in different ways. He liked to arrive five minutes late for work
and felt pleased because he was "stealing" some time from his
employer. He tried to "get" all the sex he could from his reluctant
wife because "getting a lot of sex" meant he was making up for

being cheated out of sex as an adolescent. He said he paid his therapist's bills late because it made him feel as if he was "getting something for nothing." He felt good doing these things; it meant he was "evening things out."

He described himself as "penurious," but said his wife thought he was "miserly." No purchases were made in the family without his approval. Although he made an excellent salary and his wife was employed, they enjoyed very few personal pleasures—they never went to a movie or out to dinner, and never had company.

George had come into psychotherapy shortly after his mother's death complaining of uncontrollable grief. He described symptoms of depression and anxiety—insomnia, anorexia, heart palpitations, sweating, and uncontrollable crying spells. In particular, he complained about the relationship with his wife. He felt the marriage was a constant source of hurt feelings and anger. But the most outstanding symptom was a compulsive checking pattern that got worse whenever he was under stress. Then, as if to demonstrate his compulsivity, he took from his briefcase (I quote from my comments), "piles of notes on the relationship with his wife."

I learned to respect that briefcase. George never came to therapy without it and over time he taught me to discuss whatever was listed on the legal sheets first as he was unable to talk about any other topic until we finished his list. This behavior, along with his list of symptoms, indicated that George was suffering from an obsessive-compulsive disorder (OCD) (see DSM-IV, 207).

Like many people in distress from OCD, his most troublesome symptom was checking. At night, before he went to bed, George would prowl the house for thirty or forty minutes checking doors, windows, and so forth. Never satisfied with what he had seen and heard, he would have to "check" over and over again. We made a list of all the things he had to do if he wanted to go to bed without hyperventilating. However, no matter how many times he did his rounds, his anxiety was never allayed. This is his check list:

Front door, two times; garage door, two times; laundry door, one time; downstairs toilet, one time; back room windows, one time; air conditioner, two times; back room heater, two times; stereo, two times; thermostat, three to six times; oven, three to six times (reciting to himself)," red, red, red, yellow, yellow, yellow, off, off, off" as he pressed each button; coffee pot, two times; refrigerator, two times; toaster, one time; children, three times.

George also had a handwashing compulsion and a germ phobia. When he used a public washroom he wrapped a paper towel around the door handle before touching it. When the family could convince him to go on vacation (by car; he wouldn't enter an airplane), he took with them, during the summer, winter jackets, blankets, a hot water bottle, and a thermometer—"Just in case." He had delayed one trip four hours trying to decide where to put the extra gallon of gasoline he wanted to carry, even though they would be traveling on main highways.

He and wife Brenda had two sons, sixteen and twelve. They were bright, talented children, but neither one interacted much with George, nor did he try to engage them. He complained that the oldest boy mocked him and demonstrated no respect and that the younger boy paid no attention to him.

He felt that his wife didn't love him, didn't want to be sexually intimate, had a nasty disposition, and never stopped criticizing him. She was on probation at her job because she "could not get along with her colleagues." George had similar problems at work; the group he supervised had reported many grievances about his unpleasant ("vindictive") behavior.

George also suffered from many depressive symptoms: he was anhedonic, he had lost weight, without sleeping pills he suffered from insomnia, he had little energy, and he felt depressed most of the time. A course of antidepressants helped reduce the symptoms and he said he felt better taking the meds, but all psychological issues remained.

He sat straight in his chair in his iron gray suit, white shirt, rep tie tight on his throat, no expression on his face as he recited all the stress and distress in his life. He had sought help in therapy for years, but so far he had little relief from symptoms and he had not lost any of his compulsive rituals. He sighed when he said he had little hope left.

The History: Assessment

Family Constellation and Early Recollections

George was the middle of three children who grew up in a small town in Iowa. There was a sister eight years older and a brother a few years younger. He described his sister as "a quiet, motherly sort who supposedly [sic] spent a great deal of time taking care of me."

The younger brother was George's chief competitor. Richard was handsome, popular, and charming, and any friends George had were those he shared with Richard. Describing himself as a child George said he had been

> quiet, shy, afraid of being beaten up . . . even girls could beat me up . . . afraid of failure, afraid to take risks and to do things. And I felt very self conscious about my large nose and ears. The only thing I had going for me was my intelligence.

In a later discussion he said,

> I was ugly and thought, well, the rest of me is going to be perfect even if my nose and ears aren't, so I tried to be a perfect student. [And he was.]

George described his father as a man who spent his free time drinking at a bar and watching TV. Although George felt that Father paid no attention to him ("He never taught me how to throw a ball"), his younger brother said Father often invited both boys to join him at work. Father died when George was twelve years old, leaving the family impoverished. George felt cheated again. First, looks and charm, and now, the lack of a father's love, attention, and income. His older sister was married by then and she and her husband acted *in loco parentis*. There was also a bachelor uncle who bought the children's clothes and paid all their costs through college.

The one member of the family that George adored was his mother. He described her as a good housekeeper, easy-going, pleasant, and nondemanding. He thought she "did her best" but was unappreciated by Father. Mother was a quiet, churchgoing woman who seldom complained and tried to be encouraging to her children.

Because he believed he had been "cheated" out of prosperity, George thought he had the right to take money from others by such means as stealing money from the cashbox of the grocery in which he worked, shoplifting, and taking money from his mother's purse, even though he felt guilty doing it.

His early recollections reflect his feelings of being mistreated, cheated, and disliked, and the difficulties he experienced in social situations:

Six years old: Mother took me and my cousin to the circus during school hours. The teacher found out and made me stay after school. I was sitting in the classroom by myself, the teacher had left. I felt alone and angry that I was being punished for something I really didn't do. I was being punished for having a little fun.

Eight years old: Richard and I were out in the woods. I had a pellet gun. There was another boy, Tom. Tom started running through the woods and I shot him in the back of the leg with the pellet gun. I yelled "Stop or I'll shoot," and he didn't stop. I put a red mark on his leg and he was upset and angry. I felt bad. I knew it was a foolish thing to do. I foolishly shot my own friend.

Eight years old: There was an aunt I liked who was close to my other cousins, not us. My girl cousin wrote a note to her friend in school and I intercepted the note. She wanted it back. My cousin and I went to our aunt's house and my cousin told her I had the note. My aunt forced my hand open and took the note. I was very angry at my aunt. It was none of her affair. I was hurt. It symbolized my aunt's favoritism to my cousin.

Psychodynamics

Life-style: The Social Field

The early recollections tell us that George's view of the world was one in which he expected the worst, always. For George, life was very predictable—it was always against him. In his relationship with others he believed nothing good could or would happen. Harry Sullivan writes: "The obsessional neurotic has never had the satisfaction of . . . success in interpersonal relations" (Sullivan, 1956, p. 238). George's recollections provide just such an example.

He believed he could never trust anybody as everybody was out to deprive him, to put him down, and never, ever did anybody care about *his* feelings. He felt that nobody liked him; the fact that he ate lunch alone was evidence for that. Since he never demonstrated caring or friendliness, it *was* difficult for other people to like him (the self-fulfiling prophecy). Smiling at or talking to a stranger was beyond his comprehension. Since he saw himself as awkward, it was logical on his part to be very cautious as he interacted with others. He could never act on impulse—the consequences were dreadful—and so he tried to think through every action before he made a decision about how to behave with another person. The effect of this vigilant manner was to make him appear rigid and standoffish.

Some members of his family of origin were nurturing and loving, but George did not accept them as role models. It was too important for him to believe he had been disadvantaged: he "forgot" about the generous uncle until late in therapy. He admired Mother, but imitated Father's critical ways with his own wife. Perhaps he understood that behavior as the way men behave. Possibly, in psychoanalytic language, he "identified with the aggressor" and never "resolved his Oedipal conflict." For sure, he experienced the loss of mother as being cheated again.

David Shapiro writes,

> At work, [obsessive-compulsive people] are often most comfortable feeling that they have their own little niche or bailiwick in which they devote themselves to carrying out their established duties ordained by higher authorities. . . . (Shapiro, 1965, p. 41)

George functioned well at the technical work at his office, but he had such difficulty with interpersonal relationships that he asked to be relieved of supervisory duties. If every interaction with another person has to be carefully considered and thought out, it is understandable that interpersonal behavior becomes a stress-filled chore.

Anxiety in Obsessive-Compulsive Disorders

DSM-IV lists OCD among the anxiety disorders, and anxiety and the defenses against it are the cornerstones of the psychoanalytic theories of Freud, Sullivan, Karen Horney, and the existentialists.

The Individual Psychologist understands anxiety as part of an overall arrangement in which the person creates imaginary dragons and battles them. The anxiety—the feeling that something bad is going to happen and that something has to be done to ward off the danger—is used to continue the battle. Along with anxiety, doubt and uncertainty also exist, leading the person to continually worry that whatever steps have been taken are inadequate; some danger still exists, therefore, checking the door one time is not enough. Doubt and uncertainty lead to the idea the door might not be *securely* locked. If the door is *un*locked, disaster will surely follow.

This self-created mood leads to continuous checking and rechecking of the door. Thus a small detail becomes large enough and important enough to interfere with the person's attention to the details of everyday life.

Adlerian Dynamics: The Side Show

Adler used the metaphor of the sideshow in explaining the dynamics of OCD. He understood compulsives as people who conduct their lives outside of the main ring of life; they are busy with a sideshow (an obsession or compulsion) while the rest of the world, life, takes place in the center ring.

From an Adlerian point of view George's checking is a creation, a creation of fictional monsters that makes it possible for him to do battle against the forces of evil and claim himself a courageous champion. George acted *as if* what he was doing was important. He could feel good about protecting the family from what they considered "nonsense," e.g., the summer vacations that included packing a hot water bottle, and so on,"just in case." His stance was that of a militant vigilante forced to defend himself and his family—fists up, on guard, defenses at the ready. In order to prepare for all of the bad things that might happen he had to take a multitude of precautions against the supposed impending danger.

Rituals for protecting oneself against the world are attempts to neutralize the inimical and menacing forces of nature. We see this as behavior conducted on the margins of life, drawing attention from one battlefield that is considered too big and too risky to another one small enough to handle.

In Adler's words:

> The explanation of compulsion-neurosis according to Individual Psychology . . . discloses the *unconscious purpose* of the patient [which is] to unburden and free himself by means of a compulsion from the demands made by society: [the purpose of the disorder is] to construct a subsidiary field of action in order to be able to flee from the main battle-field of life. . . . (Adler, 1968, p. 207)

We understand the obsessive-compulsive behavior as based upon the conviction that one cannot meet life without special protection. If life is seen as dangerous and unpredictable, then one cannot afford to make a mistake, one must be on guard all the time in order to spot the places where some danger might get through. In the light of these feelings it is no wonder spontaneous behavior is considered hazardous.

OCD and Responsibility

Forgus and Shulman argue that the OC person "sees himself as potentially responsible for whatever happens. . . . He stands in danger of being blamed for whatever goes wrong. His worth depends upon his ability to avoid being blamed" (Forgus & Shulman, 1979 p. 332). And Sullivan writes, "[The obsessive-compulsive] . . . cannot stand to be wrong. . . . He feels that he must not lose power over the circumstances and people with whom he is dealing, for, if he does, he will be swamped by the situation and his self-esteem . . . will be annihilated" (Chapman & Chapman, 1980, p. 121).

Once, when George and I were discussing his nightly checking habits, I asked him what would happen if his wife held a gun to his head and he couldn't check.

> GEORGE: It would be all right if she said she'd check.
> DOROTHY: But if she didn't?*
> GEORGE: Then it's her responsibility if anything goes wrong.
> DOROTHY: Could it be that if you're responsible you can be *blamed* if anything goes wrong?
> GEORGE: Yes.
> DOROTHY: What happens when you're blamed for something?
> GEORGE: I feel bad.
> DOROTHY: And then what?
> GEORGE: People will notice me.

---

*The reader will notice a difference in the designation of each therapist as in the use of "Dr. S." when Dr. Shulman is the interviewer and the use of the designation "Dorothy" when Ms. Peven is involved. The difference reflects only the difference in the style of presentation between the two therapists.

A mistake means humiliation. Others will notice him, jeer at him, scorn him, depreciate him. Others will discover how defective he really is. No man is his friend. He gives no quarter and expects no quarter.

Psychotherapy

The Goals of Therapy

One of the first goals of any therapy is to relieve suffering. George was put on a course of antidepressants and this did decrease the depressive symptoms. The relief of suffering is necessary. When clients feel better they can concentrate on what needs to be learned.

It was also important to reduce the excessive checking behavior. Yet this wouldn't happen unless George was able to feel more secure and safe without the magic rituals. The goal was to change his ideas about the world, himself, other people, and what was required for him to be more comfortable with his life.

The Course of Therapy

Shapiro (1964) believed that obsessive-compulsive people are characterized by an impairment of volitional mobility of attention. They concentrate sharply but rigidly and focus on one thing at a time. George moved slowly from one topic to another and sometimes spent a whole session on just one incident from the previous week.

Like many people who are obsessive-compulsive, he was basically a very serious person, but occasionally, George did lighten up and laugh with me. One day he took out his notes and read number one from his list, "I have made up a schedule for stopping my compulsivity." When I laughed, so did he (he got it), but he was always serious when talking about his wife.

George spent a lot of time discussing his marriage. He did take the responsibility for much of what went wrong and said it had a lot to do with his strong ideas on what women and marriage were "supposed to be like." For example, he seemed to believe that the only way he could make up for what he considered deprivation as a teenager was to "get" sex every night. So every single night he asked his wife for sex. She usually said "No" because she felt his requests as a demand, not an act of love and she didn't want to participate.

Sullivan argues:

> The obsessive-compulsive's urgent need . . . to avoid awareness of feelings . . . has various results. . . . For him "love" means the meticulous fulfillment of marital or parental obligation; his acts of "love" are devoid of tenderness and sensitivity. He behaves with brisk directness and even crudeness in many acts that should be be tender and considerate. In sexual intercourse, for instance, he often behaves with an impulsive coarseness that is devoid of sensitive collaboration. (Chapman, 1980, p. 120)

George's attitude toward sex was so greedy, so without passion, desire, tenderness, so hungry, so concerned with power rather than pleasure, and so much as if he were stealing something from his wife, I sometimes found myself feeling angry at him and would voice my displeasure. We talked about power, pleasure, the bed as a battleground for the war they had going, his attitude, and so on. He understood, and he listened carefully.

One day, while talking about himself, he said:

> I would like to know what it feels like to be in love. I've never been in love like I've seen and read about.

Could he fall in love? It would mean giving himself over to somebody else, to (figuratively) put his life in another person's hands. He had never trusted anybody to be careful of his feelings, and had never allowed himself to "let go" (as is necessary if one is to be in love). Because he focused his attention on insignificant details, George had a biased, skewed picture of events around him and missed out on many important issues in life like love and warm human relationships.

On the other hand, there were times when George understood and demonstrated considerable insight:

> Living like this enables me to be cautious and conserva-
> tive and not take a risk. To be withdrawn gives me an
> excuse to live in my own little world. I won't accept any
> risk because I never had the courage to go out and do
> things. This is what I want, . . . to have courage, but
> instead, I set up a line and say this is what I can deal with
> and across that line I can't handle it. I don't have the
> courage . . . to divorce, to reach out, to be friends and
> take the risk I might get hurt. I want to change."

George knew he had to change and he tried.

But it was hard for him. In his early twenties George had developed a growth on his nose and even though his sister urged cosmetic surgery (at her expense) on both the growth and the nose, he refused to have his nose fixed. When we discussed the psycho-logic behind his refusal of the plastic surgery, I suggested,

> Perhaps, if you had the plastic surgery you would lose
> your excuse for not being perfect. Your nose was your
> badge; your way of saying, "Look at me, I'm ugly." On
> the one hand you could say, "What do you expect from
> such an ugly man," and on the other hand, you can feel,
> "Look how far I've come in spite of my ugliness."

In order to continue to suffer George had to refuse surgery. He wanted the right to complain, to rebel, and to be noncoop-erative. George understood my interpretation and added,

> I also thought because I'm ugly I'll never get a really
> attractive woman, so I felt cheated there too.

I then asked him to finish the following sentence; "If it wasn't for my hooked nose I would. . . . [and he said] "have beautiful woman and be vice president of sales at my company." [His secret fantasies.]

Methods

As a child, George had tried to please mother. Men who want to please their mothers often strive for the approval of women therapists. During treatment with George I enlisted his desire for my approval. I affirmed his attempts to please me by giving up some of his compulsive rituals, and encouraged him to use his charm. When he allowed me, I tried to sit with him and have a sociable chat—he had so little experience with this type of social intercourse. I told George that I was getting comfortable with him, and that I found him pleasant and intelligent company.

Occasionally, I will attribute character traits to clients that are the opposite of traits displayed. If they are stingy, I compliment them on their generosity . . . if irritable, I tell them how easy they are to get along with. I call it Attribution Therapy; that is, I attribute to people those qualities that will smooth the way in human relationships and tell them they already have such and such a characteristic. I am generally greeted with quiet reflection, perhaps a smile of recognition and, more often than not, people begin to behave as if these traits *are* components of the personality. Thus, I use positive reinforcement, affirmation, and attribution of the desired behavior in the setting of a "positive transference" (a friendly relationship) to encourage and reward changes in behavior toward the desired goals.

We tried behavior modification. George put a thick rubber band on his wrist that he snapped whenever intrusive thoughts interfered with his ability to function. That helped for a while. Brenda came in with him and asked what she could do. With George's leave, we decided she should follow him around one night while he was checking. This did reduce the amount of checking but it also made George very angry.

Therapists have noted that when the symptoms of obsessive-compulsive and phobic people are interrupted, or they are forced to the phobic situation, the dreaded consequences—heart failure, panic attacks, fainting spells, and so on—do not occur. Instead, the person becomes angry, very angry because his ploy is unsuccessful. The other person has "exposed" him. Force an elevator phobic person onto an elevator and the response is cursing, not fainting. George got angry at his wife when she interfered with his checking. His anxiety did not increase.

Would group therapy help George increase his empathic ability? He attended my group. The people tried to be helpful to George, but it's not so certain George was helpful to them as he never offered sympathy, advice, or encouragement to anybody else. When asked to give an opinion or urged to discuss an issue, George turned the conversation back to himself, giving examples of his unhappy life. His behavior in the group demonstrated his inability to cooperate; he could follow the rules long enough to wait his turn, but he had no real interest in any of the other people. The group understood George and asked very little of him other than asking him to "be a little friendlier."

We encourage manners and social graces because these are social skills that facilitate good human relations, increase social acceptance, and eventually, self-esteem. The group and I were trying to demonstrate to George that if he was more pleasant, people would reciprocate. If he wore a smile, people might smile back.

Other interventions were tried. Family therapy was refused as the children would not attend. During marriage counseling sessions George regularly told his wife that he did not love her, but denied feeling antagonistic and did not understand that he hurt her feelings. As a consequence, Brenda saw no reason to modify her own behavior. But the couple insisted they wanted to stay together—for "the sake of the children," for "financial reasons," and, because divorce would be "too disruptive."

Change

George never missed an appointment, he wrote down his dreams, and he asked intelligent questions. We talked about his childhood, his family, his thoughts and feelings. I urged, he thought, and he started to transform himself. And as he changed, so did the world around him.

He began to be more loving, more tender, more considerate of Brenda's feelings and she, therefore, became more interested in sex until, finally, she approached him. He said she was getting seriously involved in their sex life and "coming on" to him and he smiled brightly.

It seems as soon as sex had no purpose other than pleasure and enjoyment and was no longer used to prove something (Peven & Shulman, 1971), George could allow more tender sexual feelings to emerge. He discovered he was not a satyr but enjoyed a normal level of desire that did not have to be gratified every night as a compulsive ritual.

He was able to reduce the amount of checking, the compulsive hand washing, and the fear of germs. At work, his performance rating went up, his boss was pleased with him, and he was acting as a supervisor again. No complaints. In fact, he started to have lunch with one of the men in his department. Brenda felt friendlier toward him, there were less conflicts, and the whole atmosphere in the house was more pleasant and cooperative.

Relapse: The Third Act

And the story would end here with a tentative "Happily ever after," but one night, on his way home from work, George's car was hit from behind by an eighteen-wheel truck. He was so seriously injured that one leg had to be amputated above the knee. Life had sabotaged him.

By chance, he was taken to the hospital with which we are associated and we made it our business to see him every day. The recovery was long and painful and he became very discouraged, especially since the skin over the stump didn't heal. He had to have skin grafts and it was not possible to fit him with a prosthesis during the months he spent in the hospital. His back had also been injured and he suffered from severe headaches. He began to feel reaffirmed in his belief that nothing good could or would ever happen to him and his behavior in the hospital reflected this.

The nurses stopped us often to complain about George's behavior:

> The IVs are never right for him. He questions us about everything we do for him. He's always worried about

germs. When we take him to the washroom he wants us to scrub the toilet before he sits down. We had to cover all the electric wires that lead from his machines. The cleaning lady won't come into his room any more, he drives her crazy.

The compulsive rituals had returned. He obsessed about the "germs" and feared contamination. He was sure infection had set in because the personnel were careless and he considered litigation against the doctors, the hospital, and the staff. He complained and criticized and finally, so did the staff.

His wife came to the hospital every day and twice a week would bring their two young sons to see him. The older boy had been disrespectful and antagonistic, but in the face of his father's injuries, he quieted and tried to be helpful.

Brenda, his wife, showed great concern and caring and did whatever she could to help him. Warned about possible fatality, Brenda convinced George to change their assets into joint tenancy. Since he never trusted anybody, including his wife, to care for his finances George had kept everything in his own name. Later, he complained that his wife had taken advantage of his illness to deprive him of his financial rights.

After several months in the hospital, George was sent home to recover. He did not have a prosthesis and found it difficult to get around on crutches. He lived in a two-story house and had trouble going up and down the stairs. He fell several times. He had trouble sitting. As time went on and winter started he became more and more reluctant to leave the house for fear of falling. He refused to do the proscribed exercises, but was compulsive in caring for the wound on his leg. Eventually he did get fitted with a prosthesis and even learned to drive again. But he was bitter . . . very bitter.

He grumbled and criticized incessantly. His obsession about the carpeting at home became so severe that he would barely move from one room to another for fear he would trip on some overlooked wrinkle in the rug. He would go out of the house only in warm weather for fear that rain or ice on the ground would cause him to slip and fall. He no longer checked the house nightly, but kept to a smaller and smaller section of the living room until his wife could no longer bear the filth surrounding him. She complained that George didn't bathe, didn't change his clothes, wouldn't take care of the household paperwork. Like many people who are obsessive-compulsive, he was untidy (and even unclean) in many of his habits; for example, he never paid his bills on time and always filed his income tax returns late. Bills were piling up and he refused to throw anything away until he was literally surrounded by newspapers and garbage.

When he felt better he wanted to start his married sex life again, but now his wife flatly refused to go near him. He complained that she had become cold and unconcerned, that their older son had started nasty teasing again, and that the younger one barely spoke to him.

I asked his wife to come in with George. She spoke of George's angry, sour behavior and said she would not have anything to do with him unless he "cleaned up his act." He refused to change anything and instead sat in the middle of the mess feeling mean and angry. Brenda became more and more frustrated, the children became more and more unpleasant, and eventually Brenda decided something had to be done. She had reached the limit of her patience. With George's reluctant consent Brenda had a contractor come in and redo the basement. A small suite was built in the basement and Brenda moved George's clothes and office down there. Peevish and miserable, George moved down to the basement.

Eventually, he stopped coming up to eat with the family and they seldom went downstairs to visit. He quit his job and went on full disability. Time passed him by . . . life passed him by . . . until his children barely remembered he was in the house and his wife made it clear she wished him out. By giving up all interaction with society George no longer experienced any defeats. He felt he had won.

He continued to believe that relationships were risky and unsatisfying. He thought it better to spend his life guarding himself while he took what he could get from an unfriendly world.

Reflections

How did George manage to convince everybody to go away?

He saw himself as a timid soul, but actually his behavior was quite hostile. He was always in silent conflict with life and other people and used concealed aggression (passive-aggressive behavior) as his method of fighting back. He was unfriendly, insensitive, unappreciative, stingy, and never expressed gratitude for anything done for him. He was neither a criminal nor a monster, but he was an unpleasant person.

Sometimes a client will evoke sympathy from the therapist and we will try harder, persist, give more positive feedback, more validation. It wasn't easy to like George, but he was not a "bad boy." He was a man who was limited, sick, and suffering. And, before the accident, George was trying so hard it was motivating to me.

Immediately after the accident George and Brenda were able to cooperate. As the months wore on and George reverted to his compulsive behavior, the relationship worsened and they returned to their old ways.

The people in the group called him both from group meetings and from home, expressing sympathy and best wishes for a quick recovery. George would mumble a polite thank you, but never asked after the welfare of others.

What is the significance of the return of symptoms . . . the obsessive-compulsive behavior? One way of understanding it is that the stress of the accident precipitated the use of George's old coping behavior. He was just trying to be safe, to get life back under control so that he could handle it. He truly believed that by giving up his security behavior, by not being vigilant enough, he had precipitated the accident.

Sometimes the gains a person makes are not established well enough to withstand the vicissitudes of severe stress. George's terrible accident is such an example. Under such circumstances people often go back to a more familiar coping style.

Furthermore, people who spend so much time trying to be safe will use behavior that is unsafe. George was a terrible driver—more than once he told me how he questioned his driving decisions and how once he had even made a U-turn in the middle of a busy street. Not only did he believe that he had been cheated and that life was inimical to him, but he also had mistaken notions about what the real dangers in life actually are.

Epilogue

In focusing his attention on insignificant details, George, like many obsessive-compulsive people, did not actually observe what was going on around him and missed out on the really important issues in life, like love and warm human relationships. He became like an automaton, living out his life in pointless acts of ritualistic behavior. Life held little joy, playfulness, or spontaneity.

The last I heard of George he was living in the basement, not wearing his prosthesis, afraid to go out—depressed, bitter, isolated, and neglected, complaining that he was doomed to be unlucky, deprived, and cheated.

—D. Peven

References

Adler, A. (1968). *The practice and theory of individual psychology.* New York: Littlefield, Adams & Co.

American Psychiatric Association. (1994). *Diagnostic and Statistical Manual of Mental Disorders* (4th ed.). Washington, DC: Author.

Chapman, A. & Chapman, M. (1980). *Harry Stack Sullivan's concepts of personality development and psychiatric illness.* New York: Brunner Mazel.

Forgus, R., & Shulman, B. H. (1979). *Personality: A cognitive view.* Englewood Cliffs, NJ: Prentice-Hall, Inc.

Shapiro, D. (1965). *Neurotic styles.* New York: Basic Books.

Shulman, B. H., & Peven, D. E. (1971). Sex for domination. *Medical Aspects of Human Sexuality,* 5(10), 28–32.

Sullivan, H.S. (1956) Clinical studies in psychiatry. In H. Perry, M. Gawel, & M. Gibbon (Eds.), *Clinical studies in psychiatry.* New York: W. W. Norton.

4

Who
Is Sylvia?

Who is Silvia? what is she?
—William Shakespeare,
Two Gentlemen of Verona, act 4, scene 2.

Following my usual custom with new patients, I went into the waiting room to introduce myself to Sylvia. She was sitting upright, wearing dark blue sunglasses, a trench coat, boots, and a hat. She stood up to meet me and followed me into the consultation room. She sat down on the other side of the desk, hands in lap, legs crossed, and did not take off her coat or sunglasses. Watching her guarded behavior, the way in which she sat in her chair, the fact that she did not take off her sunglasses or coat, suggested to me that I be cautious in my approach to her. I surmised that questioning would be considered intrusive, therefore, I deliberately let her tell her story in any way she chose. I was particularly careful since she had been referred to me by her internist after she made a suicide attempt.

She spoke freely, and told me that although she had been depressed the whole forty-five years of her life, the past six months had been worse than usual. She had been seeing a psychiatrist during this period and told me a vague story about how she was beginning to trust him until he told her he was planning to go away for the summer. This seemed an odd reason to distrust, but she claimed that this upset her so much she stopped seeing him.

Taking a careful history was tedious. Sylvia's answers were

seldom precise. She knew that she wanted to die, that "life was not worth living," but she no longer had a desire to kill herself. She slept well, with the help of a sleeping pill, but often did not get out of bed all day. She could not concentrate enough to read a book or watch TV. "Everything" was "hard to do." She had stopped driving, but her mother took her wherever necessary. Even though she had her own apartment, she stayed at her parents' house most of the time. She maintained few social contacts, would visit family with her parents, had fewer and fewer interests and felt more and more unable to change her life or her behavior.

Ten years before she had moved to and worked in Los Angeles and for a short while she appeared to function well and was enjoying herself. But then she had a brief psychotic episode, perhaps brought on by taking diet pills. She had delusions that "others" had malicious intent and were going to harm her. The episode cleared in a few weeks, but left her very unsure of herself. She had been treated for depression many times in the past, but was critical of her past treatment. She felt none of her previous analysts were "competent." They "didn't understand" her.

At the time she came to see me, she was taking diet pills (again) and a tranquilizer. The latter helped her to sleep, the former, to control her body weight. She was also taking an antidepressant at bedtime. Her use of this last medication was irregular and she often did not take it for days at a time. Therefore, at the end of the first session, in light of the fact of her excessively guarded experience, her complaints about her previous therapists, and her recent suicide attempt, I told her that I would leave it up to her to decide whether or not she would return to see me.

Three weeks passed. Her internist called and asked me if I would see Sylvia again. When she came in she told me she was ashamed to call herself, feeling she had offended me. I reviewed the situation with her and told her I believed she needed medication for the depressive symptoms, but had to agree to use the medication properly. I told her that if she could not be completely frank with me that there was little chance I could help her.

She told me that she always felt inferior to others and gave examples: she had not been a good student and believed she could not drive a car well. It seemed she had acquired a whole list of activities to which she could point claiming she could not do any of these things as well as others. Her collection of inadequacies seemed insufficient to explain how deeply inferior she felt. After all, most of us do not claim inferiority if we are not racecar drivers or Mensa members. This seemed to be an exaggerated sensitivity to supposed deficiencies that most people would not consider significant.

Background

As Sylvia talked about her history she said that "even as a child" she felt that her "needs were never met." Her father was the CEO of a large company and appeared to be much respected and admired by the community. As a child, she stood in awe of him and even somewhat frightened. He had been "uninvolved," had never played with her or had physical contact with her. He appeared to be angry when she approached him and she often felt that Father disapproved of her. He was a very critical man who found fault with everything and everybody, telling her, for instance, that all any therapist wanted was to "collect money."

She had a younger sister who seemed to be the apple of Mother's eye—she was married to a successful lawyer and had two children. Sylvia felt fondly toward her and did appreciate her sister's interest in her, but she admitted that she often felt jealousy and envy. Her sister seemed to have everything Sylvia wanted. As children, Sister had outdistanced Sylvia in every area of importance to Sylvia, which contributed to her feelings of inferiority.

She described Mother as "passive and long-suffering," and said she could not respect her mother because she had let Father dominate her. She thought Mother was "dumb" and "inadequate." The atmosphere in the house was critical and distant and family members did not show physical or verbal affection for each other. Faultfinding and judging others was the norm. In fact, she believed that Father considered her worthless and Mother disliked her for all the "trouble" she had caused. (She had been seeing psychiatrists since she was twelve.) I understood that she felt that no one in the family had made her feel loved, wanted, or worthy and that she had received no information that made her feel good about herself.

In the absence of what seemed to be genuine caring, Sylvia believed her parents had a loveless relationship. Father's superior, critical attitude and Mother's passive tolerance and distance from Father contributed to a frigid atmosphere in the house. Neither seemed to cherish the other or their children.

Sylvia never felt she "counted" to Mother who took great pleasure in Sister's accomplishments. On the other hand, recently, Father seemed to enjoy her company; he would talk to her for long periods explaining his cynical philosophy of life. Nevertheless, she also considered Father to be cruel in his criticism and disapproval of her, and Mother would not defend her.

"Mother let him come first. If you didn't turn yourself off to it [Father's treatment of Mother], it was pretty demoralizing." She recalled feeling as a child that "things are going to fall apart," and associated this with the feeling she had about the relationship between her parents. In fact, she worried constantly that her parents were going to divorce and she would be left "alone."

Although Mother did more for her than Father, Sylvia always felt that Mother considered it a chore. She did not feel like a source of joy or pride to her parents. However, she felt liked by her peers and could experience positive feelings with them. But she never felt close to anybody, nor did she ever share her thoughts and feelings. She explained that she protected herself by keeping distance—"I can't get hurt if I don't love."

In college, Sylvia had dated several young men who were attracted to her, but she never felt that they were "good enough" and she would look down on them and drop them (if they didn't drop her first for her constant criticisms). She felt used (and abused) by all men and believed that she had failed in every relationship starting with Mother and Father and progressing until the present. She said she had never "understood" relationships and did not know how to make them work.

She had had a love affair with a married man she found "irresistible" and had spent five years in a stormy relationship with him until his wife discovered the affair and forced him to make a choice. She said she felt "relieved" at the end because she had felt so tortured about the relationship. Since then there had been no sexual relationships and very little dating.

History

Eventually, Sylvia began to tell me about the events of the year prior to her suicide attempt. She had been employed for six years at a bank, and was doing a good job. Then she decided to go to school and further her education. She enrolled in a finance class, but had no strong motivation to study and so she became discouraged and dropped the class. This served to prove to her that she was inadequate. She saw no future at the bank and decided to quit the job and take a world tour. (Father was wealthy and she never had to worry about money.) On the tour she noticed that other people seemed to be in couples while she was alone and she found herself missing her previous lover, although she had not seen him for years.

When she returned from the trip, she "knew" that she "had to die" rather than live alone for the rest of her life. "I don't recall wanting to die, but I wanted to change something in my life." So she attempted suicide. She told me she had started planning the suicide the previous year, saving up the medication her doctor gave her.

> After I got back from my trip, I had nothing to look forward to, nothing I could do, I began to get depressed and kind of decided that I would never come out of the depression. Eventually, I wouldn't get out of bed. I felt frozen. There was nothing inside me. I was coming to my appointments as a frozen person, . . . so I saved up my meds and took them all at once. I was shocked when I woke up in the hospital. And terrified. Caged in. A nightmare. . . .

"How do you feel about it now?" I asked. She answered, speaking slowly,

I've had a lot of psychiatrists and nobody has really helped me. I am hoping that you are competent, that you know what you are doing.

Transference and Countertransference

Not only did Sylvia feel inferior, she projected her feelings onto others and believed others considered her worthless. She said she was a "false front with nothing behind it," but she had enough insight to know that her distrust of others resulted from her own feeling of worthlessness. When the behavior of others seemed to verify this, it evoked anger in her. Thus, if I were late to a session, she thought it indicated my disregard for her.

I did not contest her complaints and admitted that I was sometimes late. I listened to her expressions of anger and told her I would do my best, would give her a different time slot, and apologized for my lateness. She was not mollified. She had many angry outbursts at me; afterwards, she would apologize and express appreciation for my putting up with her. I used one of these occasions to make an interpretation—that behind her "front" was a great deal of anger and hurt and sadness that had held her back in life and that helping her to feel worthwhile was an important task for me.

I found Sylvia intriguing. She was often angry with me, but she never failed to keep an appointment. I wanted to understand why she had not left me, just as she had all her other analysts. What attracted her to me? I would ask and she would give different answers at different times. One time she stated that I seemed cool and distant and she took this as a sign that I knew what I was doing. On another occasion she said she appreciated my ability to put up with her temper.

My own choice of behavior with Sylvia grew out of my intuitive reaction to this type of behavior on the part of a patient. It seemed to me that she was watching me for any sign of incompetence or insensitivity so that I would become just another therapist who couldn't help her. It is my policy at such challenges to inform my patient that I have many faults. What she could count on was that I would do my best, but when she found my mistakes she would have to excuse me for them.

I never disliked Sylvia, but I never felt any real warmth toward her. There were times when I felt sympathetic and sorry for what she was going through, but I always felt that it was important that certain boundaries never be crossed; for example, I was very careful never to display in speech or behavior any erotic interest. In the first place, I didn't feel any erotic interest in her, and, in the second place, I was very concerned that she would misinterpret any move on my part to be "closer."

I reviewed the feelings she had for me, but I did not ask or suggest that she might have romantic or erotic feelings toward me although I believed she did. However, I would not bring up the subject nor interpret any of her behaviors in that direction. I was concerned that any interpretation of that nature would lead Sylvia down a path she would be too frightened to take. And I did not want to provoke her in that direction. I felt that her defensive behavior was paranoid and I went out of my way to avoid statements that could be interpreted with a double meaning.

Ethics aside, she needed distance from me, and she needed to know that no matter her interest in me, I would not take advantage of her. She had to feel *safe* with me in order for us to do psychotherapy.

Sylvia admitted she was surprised by my willingness to admit my own flaws and apologize for them. My attitude of "one doesn't have to be perfect to be worthwhile" seemed to impress her. Her admiring remarks made me cautious, because I did not think it would be helpful for her to idealize me; rather, it would be more useful to her to be able to believe that ordinary people could have weaknesses and still be liked and appreciated.

Sylvia and I spent a considerable amount of time discussing our relationship. Her feelings toward me reawakened many of the feelings she had both for her father and her mother. Sylvia's social circle included her mother, her father, me, and, peripherally, her sister. Therefore, most discussions centered on her feelings toward these people. For example, during a discussion of the way in which her parents did not understand her feelings, Sylvia said her relationship with me as a therapist seemed to work because I was treating her "the way I wanted to be treated all my life." I understood that to mean that I validated her subjective apperceptions.

Soon after she said, "I have had psychiatrists all my life like some people have dentists," and added that she preferred working with me because I seemed "cold and businesslike" and she believed that was what she needed. I was a little surprised by this comment because I had imagined that I was being attentive and kind. Furthermore, she had chosen to sit on the chair that was farthest away from my desk, and I had simply accepted her arrangement. I pointed this out to her and she admitted that she was keeping her distance (she was still wearing the blue sunglasses that hid her eyes, a coat, and often, a hat).

In the first few months of psychotherapy, I had some difficulty understanding certain core aspects of her personality because I had never insisted on structuring any interview with her. That is, I never collected formal life-style information. I felt she had been exposed to too much of the wrong kind of structuring in the past and that she needed to feel that it was alright for her to move forward at her own speed and tell me only what she was prepared to reveal. She had easily accepted the outer structures of psychotherapy; she came to sessions on time and had a check written out beforehand.

Actually, I did not trust Sylvia. On the one hand, she sincerely wanted help; on the other hand, her script was one in which she expected disappointment, and I didn't want to be the antagonist in her drama. I could appreciate that she had not developed an inner sense of self-worth (for which she blamed her parents) and her posture as critic and faultfinder was both a defense against rejection and a compensatory depreciation of others. She was giving herself the right to demand total competence from me and also protecting herself from any demands I might make. I could see why her relationships with men had all ended in rupture.

At times when patients are defensive, angry, and critical, I will listen, show interest, ask about possible connections, refer to the past, but will make few interpretations. I noted also that Sylvia

displayed a behavior often seen in patients who resist interpretation. Whenever I asked if she felt such and such, she would
have to change my language—her description was presented
always as more accurate than mine.

Although she calmed down a little as time went by, she still
became angry with me if I was even a minute late. But then she
would comment quickly that she appreciated my accepting her
anger. Whereas she had previously seen my behavior as insensitive, eventually she saw it as an unfortunate inconvenience that
happened in spite of good intentions. She commented that
although she would flare up, she could not stay angry with me
and confessed that she liked me and wanted me to like her, and
could not understand why she had reacted so intensely when I
didn't behave the way she wanted.

About three months into therapy I asked Sylvia to report
dreams and she did. They were short dreams, all about my
office or me. In the dreams, she was always a spectator, always
observing my behavior, thinking about it, commenting on it. She
was busy negotiating appointments with me, or coming into my
office, or waiting for me. We discussed these dreams as comments
about her feelings toward me.

Her anger was a constant subject. She said she tried to stop
being angry, but could not. She was frightened by this and called
it "a craziness inside of me—an evil." But she also knew that
she projected this feeling onto others; when she became enraged,
she would believe that "others" were malevolent to her,
including me.

> Part of me really likes you and wants to give things to
> you and a part of me wants to discredit you.

She was always afraid that she would destroy the relationship
with me. Asked to explain, she said she feared that her suspicious, distrustful, (paranoid) thoughts and feelings would return
and she would become unable to trust me. She thought that,
eventually, her " thoughts" would bring about the end of the
relationship with me and then she would make another suicide
attempt.

I assured her that I would not allow her to anger me to the point at which I would refuse to see her any longer, nor would I ever be able to be all the things she wanted me to be. She admitted she wanted my appreciation and admiration and that she became furious if she thought I was overlooking her.

After about a year Sylvia began to bring me little presents—a post-it pad with my name printed on it, a golf ball, a valentine, and a copy of a review of one of my books. I discussed this with her without rejection, devaluation, or criticism. I expressed my pleasure, admired the present, and appreciated the effort she had made. Sylvia would smile and say that she was glad I understood how careful she had been to pick out "just the right thing" for me.

Whether I agreed with her taste or not, I wanted to validate her. I believe validation is one of the most healing things a therapist can do for a person with feelings of inferiority and alienation. Validation recognizes, accepts, respects, and honors the person as the "other," a reification of the other's identity. It is probably very close to Martin Buber's concept of the I-Thou relationship.

Sylvia was nothing if not ambivalent, and this characteristic appeared in many aspects of her life. For example, on the one hand she said she "cared" about me, and on the other hand she continued to say things like, "I still don't trust you or even like you." I understood that as her attempt to keep sufficient distance between the two of us to let her feel nonthreatened.

The most common emotion Sylvia experienced was anger and I was usually the recipient. Once I changed the time of her appointment and she felt "betrayed." Another time, she was in the waiting room when a young woman patient, whom I had known since she was a child, hugged me before she left. Sylvia felt I should not have let this happen. She continually reminded me of how I had been late, been interrupted, changed her session time, and let a patient hug me. Throughout her expressions I had been constant, accepting her anger, saying I was sorry she was offended, but that was the kind of practice I had, and I could only try my best not to offend her.

"I know you are sensitive," I said, "but I may not always be, and you may have to tell me if I am insensitive."

She answered; "I want you to be more serious about my case. I want you to corroborate me."

"Do I not do enough of that?" I asked.

"I feel it doesn't count if I have to remind you to do it."

Before I left town on a trip, she sent me a card with a humorous remark—"Have a good time. Don't think about how miserable I will be while you're gone"—and a comic cartoon of a lonely puppy. I sent her a postcard while I was away and she later told me, "I felt treasured."

But this didn't stop her from expressing her anger at me for being insensitive, for not treating her with the "special care" she felt she needed. She was jealous of every other patient and every other therapist in my office. And her dreams portrayed her feelings:

> I dreamed I was walking in a seamy part of town. One side of the street was sunny and cheerful and you were standing there. I felt I was on the dark side. You waved to me to come over to your side. The look on your face was the way I see you when I'm thinking the worst about you or when I don't believe something you are saying. . . .

Then she interpreted her own dream.

> Trust is such a big problem for me. . . . I never used to trust anybody. Now I feel I have to trust you to keep getting well. You really have to bear with me. There's something difficult about the neighborhood we're in right now."

The "Thoughts": Paranoia

The dream sounded somewhat psychotic to me and I began to think of Sylvia as paranoid. If I thought of her as having paranoid thoughts, her behavior made sense—the sunglasses, the coat, the cautious distance-keeping behavior—all had the purpose of self-protection. Suspicious thoughts and distrustful feelings were the natural companions of this intention. The end result was social distance and dysphoria, a critical, disapproving, self-protective attitude toward the world.

She then described one experience she had had with an early boyfriend who grew tired of her persistent demands and broke off the relationship. Sylvia described herself as having the feeling that the "thoughts had become a reality" and that the thoughts themselves were a "destructive force" that came from her. "I don't want to have the thoughts anymore," she said.

I asked to her to consider that the thoughts themselves might best be considered as a symptom of anxiety and that if we examined the sources of her anxiety, we might be able to identify how the thoughts actually came about. She said she was aware that she was inappropriately suspicious and felt embarrassed by it.

> SYLVIA: It seems so stupid to be so embarrassed, but it happens. . . . I have no control over my thought process.
> DR. S: What will happen if you cannot control your thoughts? Who has betrayed you so badly in the past that you are afraid to trust? And why are you afraid that you will have to go to the hospital again?

She could not answer, but said she had decided to trust me, and that it felt "Miraculous that it had happened." My notes of the session say:

> Today she expresses her feelings more clearly and with understanding. She doesn't like being vulnerable, and wants safety and the feeling of being cared for. She recalled that after our first session, she felt that I knew what I was doing and this helped her to feel safe.

In the next few weeks, Sylvia reported that she "felt good" and credited me with helping her. But, after two weeks, the good feelings were gone. She had overslept, missed an appointment, and someone who was supposed to call her had not done so. I was now able to connect the occurrence of the "thoughts" with a feeling of frustration that occurred when inconvenient and unwanted events took place, and I said, "You seem to believe that these small oversights, mistakes and so on set off an alarm that says something bad has happened, that you are in danger." She did not respond.

At the next session a remarkable thing happened. She found Lawrence Kolb's chapter on paranoid psychoses in the library (Kolb, 1982) and brought me a copy, underlined everywhere she thought was significant. She recalled and described her paranoid episode in California and recognized that there had been two other occasions when she had been psychotic. She said she was beginning to understand that her hostile, angry stance was not really a form of strong defense, but a form of "madness." She recalled being very frightened, becoming agoraphobic, and afraid to leave her apartment. She simply stopped seeing whatever therapist was helping her during those times.

She wanted assurance that I would recognize when she was so disturbed ("sick") that she felt fragile and unable to tolerate behavior on my part that might touch a raw nerve. I again told her I could tolerate her anger and keep her safe, and that I would not let her drive me away.

The Past: Psychotherapy

Now I felt ready to probe the past and asked for incidents where events of frustration had happened. I encouraged her to look into memories of the past. She remembered that as a child she was always angry. She would have screaming arguments with her parents accusing them of being "mean" and "not loving her." Although she never engaged in actual physical attacks she would throw herself on the floor and bang her hands and feet. All of her memories of childhood were about anger, jealousy, and rage at being treated in an unacceptable way.

She still felt "deprived" by Mother, was always angry with her, and would find fault and start arguments. Feeling guilty she would buy her mother presents to make up. But I knew Sylvia's view was inaccurate since Sylvia herself had told me of the many times Mother had gone out of her way to do things for Sylvia such as driving her to sessions when Sylvia felt too timid to drive.

I did not contradict Sylvia openly, but approached what I thought was a misapperception from another angle. I began to speculate, out loud, wondering if her parents ever really understood her. Perhaps she was a puzzle to them and they really didn't know how to deal with her. I wanted her to reflect on what I said. And she did.

She said that this speculation was "satisfying" because it seemed to explain her past to her. She started to consider that perhaps her parents never knew how she felt, did not realize that she was too frightened and confused to complain and did not feel that complaining or showing her fears were an option. She felt that her parents treated her as if she had no right or reason to complain.

All this time she had been living with her parents. Eventually, she began to talk about moving back to her own apartment. Again she was experiencing ambivalence. She felt that moving out in order to be on her own would be a venture back into the world, but she found reasons not to leave her parents: they were "old," they "needed" her, they would "worry" about her. She avoided discussing her own fears until I gently confronted her by suggesting that she was using the thought "I don't want to upset them" as a justification for not doing what she needed to do. Ambivalence, after all, is often a mental device for avoiding initiating an action.

I suggested that we deal openly with her fear, acknowledge it and examine it. Sylvia did not like what I said and responded by speaking in sentences with numerous dependent clauses and successfully avoided the issue. But, she said, she realized that she had become irritable and quarrelsome with her parents and had even accused them of trying to push her out. She even saw an analogy between the way in which she dealt with her parents and the way in which she had dealt with her relationships with men.

This was a significant insight for her. Whereas, in the past, she had simply seen quarrels and disagreements without any understanding of her own role in the fights, now she was able to see that her behavior had precipitated the ending of her relationships. She saw her quarrels with Mother as *her* problem and she realized that this is what she had also done with men. Here was a demonstration of displacement: she had to do something to appease the turbulence of the moment and what she chose to do was to fight.

She became able to see herself as having two patterns of thinking—one in which there was a rational explanation for whatever happened, and the other in which she believed she was being mistreated. She then began to discuss the one relationship she had had with the married man. She described her insecurity, her quarrelsomeness, and her uncertainty about sexual inter-course. She had never experienced orgasm during intercourse.* In fact, when the relationship was over, it was almost a relief from the constant tension.

Progress

In time, Sylvia began to feel more free, less concerned with her fear of doing something that would incur disapproval and she began to want social relationships with men again. She met an older, unmarried man in the mailroom of her building and struck up a conversation with him. Soon, she began to spend time with him. She felt appreciated by him and enjoyed his company.

He seemed interested in her and she began to have some erotic fantasies about him. One thing she said she liked about him was that he had a tendency to "take charge," but this also alarmed her. She was afraid that if she allowed herself to become more intimate with him, she would begin to lose control of her own emotions and would repeat her past painful relationships.

"At what point," I asked her, would she feel she had "lost control?" She explained that as soon as she would declare her attraction, she would feel she was at his mercy and would begin to behave in needy ways. As a result, she believed it would be better for her not to enter into a closer relationship.

She began to see her anger as a response to anticipated threat, a way of protecting herself and keeping distance from those who

---

*Women who do not "trust" often have difficulty achieving orgasm.

might hurt her. If she liked someone (using me as her example) she felt that this empowered the other person and left her vulnerable. But she could see that these feelings interfered with her ability to enjoy her life.

Soon after this revelation she discovered that she could be with her parents without feeling anger. In fact, she learned she could influence the way they treated her by the way she treated them. It was a newfound strength she never knew existed and it felt "wonderful."

However, she would still express anger at me for being tardy, for being "insensitive," for not treating her with the "special care" she felt she needed. She would still become jealous if she saw me greet another client in the waiting room: "You have to remember how painful it can be for me." And then she brought in a dream, which portrayed her mixed feelings:

> I was sitting in a church listening to a popular preacher. The other people began drifting out of the church and I thought that I didn't want to be the last one out. I tried to leave but I couldn't get the door open. The preacher told me that he was keeping me as a hostage. My first impulse was to kick and scream, but I thought that would only make me more frightened, so I decided to resign myself. We got in a car and drove to a ball park and up a high ramp where I got frightened again and then I became resigned again. Other people were sitting in the ballpark and trying to exchange me for a nuclear scientist. I decided that the government would never exchange an important person for me, so I would be killed anyway. . . .

Sylvia was surprised that in her dreams she so quickly could turn from panic to resignation. She wondered if I would interpret the dream as showing suicidal feelings. I did not. We had been talking in the previous session about power and feelings of powerlessness and I interpreted the dream as the change in her ability to control her own feelings, even though it seemed to put her under someone else's power.

I also saw this dream as, again, about the relationship with me. It seemed to be an announcement that even though she might fall hostage to me, she was going to accept the situation and face whatever frightening outcome followed. She did not believe she could be important enough for me and the government (or anybody) to rescue her.

I continued to reformulate Sylvia's ideas, beliefs, values, and thoughts. She believed that she was "sensitive" and this caused interpersonal problems for her (e.g., with Mother, Father, friends). I suggested to her that perhaps it would be more useful to approach this from a reverse view; namely, that interpersonal problems cause her to be "sensitive." In this way, she would have to accept responsibility for her sensitivity. This struck a chord in Sylvia. She recalled that a previous therapist had once told her that she didn't even accept responsibility for her own thoughts.

Sylvia was able to carry this idea into her discussions of her relationship with her parents. She could now describe incidents in which her attempts to be helpful and considerate had been unrewarded. She told me, "The nicest thing you ever said to me was when you told me you noticed the changes in me and felt proud of me. No one was ever proud of me."

She described herself as becoming less of a detective, more able to hear what I was saying, understand it, and feel less defensive. She found herself accepting the language I used and less likely to want to correct my way of making interpretations. Sylvia experienced the realization that she had tried to depend on an unreliable, unhappy, and unrewarding mother, instead of developing her own internal resources. She felt liberated and she now knew in what direction she had to move. "I always thought it was my problem. . . . I thought my background was good, so it must be my fault."

One day Sylvia came to a therapy session in standard transparent glasses rather than her blue sunglasses. She still wore a coat and a long skirt, but she wasn't wearing a hat. I was pleased and took this as a positive sign of progress.

Soon after she asked for an extra appointment on the same day. I told her I had no later openings, but would stay later and see her at the end of the day. She refused. Later, she told me how she had described this to her male friend, saying that she felt I was depreciating her and making her feel guilty for asking. She was surprised when her friend said he thought I was being kind and considerate to her. It struck her that this was an example of how she was transferring, investing me with behavior that she perceived in her parents.

Another day she brought me a box of candy that I set out in the waiting room for all comers. She then accused me of not appreciating her generosity, not prizing her gifts, liking other patients better, and so on. By this time I felt free to use more humor with her, and I would say that perhaps she was right in her accusations and I would try to do better because I understood she had a terrible fear of rejection and depreciation.

She became less angry with her parents, less likely to attribute hostile motives to others and to recognize that anger and unexpressed hostility to others had been a defense she had used to conceal her actual feelings of helplessness and loneliness. She was spending weekdays at her own apartment and weekends with her parents. And this arrangement also suited her relationship with her older male friend. She was aware that she was not in love with him, and therefore did not have to struggle with strong emotions. She enjoyed the relationship and could engage in intimacy and then separate from him, but she was still troubled with anger, guilt, and anxiety while with her parents and still occasionally argued with them. But, it was better. The difference between the past and the present was startling to her. She was able to see a friendly enjoyable companionship as a possible future.

Commentary

When people avoid intimate relationships because they will "get hurt," they are avoiding one particular task of life. These people often do not like the emotional and physiological arousal that comes with closeness and intimacy, especially falling in love. They are overly concerned with the feelings of "loss of control" and will begin to behave in ways that will drive others away. They avoid emotional arousal because it is unpleasant for them and alarming, so they begin the "thinking" that leads to avoidance. They tell themselves cautionary statements such as "I'm nervous and I won't say the right thing. I'll look like a fool. I'll mess it up." They create a cascade of cognitions that lead to avoidance behavior by exaggerating the dangers and depreciating the hoped-for benefits.

The concept of a "cascade" is useful here. Each thought leads to another more frightening thought until the desired emotional attitude is achieved. It is a "pep *rout*" rather than a "pep *rally*." From a therapeutic point of view, we see the person's behavior as: "I'm afraid, therefore I will avoid." The opposite point of view is: "Do it, get hurt, get over it!" I couldn't push Sylvia that hard, but I did encourage her to put her toe in the water.

It seemed to me that Sylvia was changing through the therapeutic use of the transference. She acted out her paranoid fears and her wishes for appreciation in her relationship with me. Her behavior then gave me the opportunity to suggest alternative points of view while I created an environment in which she could feel validated and safe. Albert Stone writes,

> A positive transference and a sense of new possibilities are, I believe, an essential element of any helping relationship. Being a participant in a human encounter calls on the therapist's interpersonal skills of engagement in a way that analytic neutrality does not. . . . My focus in therapy is not to make insightful interpretations; rather, the goal is to empower the patient for change. [This means] . . . the patient can try to do something differently and be rewarded, reinforced and strengthened by the responses of significant others. . . . The key to my response is to be a supporting and encouraging master—only the patient can change his or her life and this means he or she has to do something differently. . . . (Stone, 1987)

Paranoia

Paranoid personality disorder (see DSM-IV, p. 276) has as its main feature distrust and suspicion. People with this disorder behave as if they are surrounded by enemies who will do them harm. Therefore, they are constantly on guard. Paranoid people must conceal their own vulnerabilities and find the vulnerabilities of others in order to know the weakness of the enemy. Interpersonal relationships are the battlefield since all people are understood as malevolent.

The paranoid personality has an incidence of 0.52 to 2.5 percent in the population (DSM-IV, p. 276). People with the disorder rarely come for treatment because they seldom believe they are in need of treatment. The condition is also characterized by brief psychotic episodes, and Sylvia did have several episodes lasting a few days that were characterized by confusion, delusional thinking, and intense fear.

But paranoia also has some survival value. If somebody believes that "they are out to get me," it may make sense to attack first. Taking aggressive action can make the person feel strong and powerful, able to defeat the enemy. Anger overcomes fear, and anger is a more comfortable emotion to live with than fear.

As time went on I was able to introduce my thoughts to Sylvia by prefacing my remarks with "Now this will give you a chance to feel paranoid and get angry but there is something I want to point out to you ..." She was amused by this, took it as a genuine attempt on my part to be considerate, and was able to listen without her automatic rage response.

What Sylvia had to learn was to live her life without having to feel superior, without measuring herself against others and to live without having to keep her guard up. By exaggerating petty concerns she was actually avoiding real challenges, making everyday activities too hard to do. It would be more effective for her to just do the things she had to do without trying to do them perfectly. She needed what Dr. Rudolf Dreikurs used to call the "courage to be imperfect."

Validation

Suddenly, Sylvia's father had a heart attack and was hospitalized. He was treated and seemed to be improving when he had a repeat attack and died. The grieving, difficult for any child, was especially so for Sylvia. Yet she was, at this time, able to see

Mother's strength, her ability, although grief-stricken, to handle the arrangements and console Sylvia. But the most striking aftermath of Father's death was Sylvia's discovery that her supposedly superior father, who seemed critical and disapproving of everyone else, especially of Mother, had not left a will. This was a shock to Sylvia; perhaps her critical Father was not truly competent and superior after all. Sylvia began to see that it was Mother who had run the house and actually made most of the decisions. When she thought about it, she realized Father had only read the paper and made critical remarks.

It was as if this allowed Sylvia to free herself from the childhood fears of disapproval. Her parents, after all, seemed much less powerful now. If they had not been good parents to her it was not because they were malicious, but rather, imperfect. Mother tried to validate her, but did not know how. Father had been a prejudiced man who had loved her, but saw people only from his own cynical and suspicious point of view. Sylvia began to feel pity for her parents. But even if she was wrong about Mother being malicious, the important thing for her to learn was to stop the angry behavior, to accept instead of being judgmental.

I used a story to try to teach her:

DR. S: A mother is feeding a child, but the mother doesn't see very well and the spoon keeps missing the child's mouth. What does the child think?

SYLVIA: The mother is doing it on purpose!

DR. S: What does the child need to do? The child cries and complains but mother still can't find the mouth. The child is angry and hates Mother but nothing changes. What should the child do?

SYLVIA: The child has to change it's own behavior. It has to stop expecting food from mother and learn to rely on itself. I will have to rely on myself.

DR. S: Can you do it?

SYLVIA: I think so.

She then took over the management of the estate with a bank to help her.

Aware of feeling much freer and happier, she often wondered if the happiness would last. She realized she could not rely on Mother for happiness and, if she wanted to continue to feel happy, that she would have to participate more in the world as it was and spend less time finding faults in others and less effort in perfect task performance endeavors. She started to remind herself that she did not want to be the disapproving judge that Father was or waste time in raging at the behavior of those who disappointed her.

Fortuitously, Sylvia found outside validation of what she was learning. An estate lawyer reviewed the situation and told her that her father had actually used poor judgment and her mother was not able to understand the complexities of the situation as well as Sylvia could. This was a rare compliment for Sylvia who rarely did anything to give another person a chance to evaluate her performance. It gave her a feeling of confidence greater than she had had before.

We identified and listed the stratagems she was still using that interfered with her ability to have a positive self-image.

1. When she feels good about something she does, she depreciates it. (Father's behavior)
2. When she prepares for plans to do something, she predicts failure to herself. (Father's predictions)
3. She looks for obstacles and magnifies them. (Discourages herself)
4. She sabotages her own motivation by doubting the accuracy of her observations. (She can't believe she might actually be intelligent)

For us, this is an important part of the therapeutic process and we want patients to learn to introspect like this. Thinking like this led Sylvia to see the sequence of events that led to paranoid feelings and thoughts. These feeling and thoughts would occur regularly and automatically in certain specific situations, which we could now identify because they were happening much less often.

The paranoid thoughts and feelings seemed to be a learned

behavioral response to a conditioned stimulus; in this case the conditioned stimulus was *any unexpected event* (e.g., a therapist takes a vacation or moves his office), which then is perceived by her as an insult, a rejection, or neglect.

Termination

Sylvia was much less depressed now. She was handling Father's estate. She was more tolerant of Mother. She felt safer with me, trusting that I was an ally. She began to think about taking school classes, was meeting more people, and was enjoying a feeling of satisfaction with herself that she had never experienced before. She was enjoying her semi-intimate relationship with her male friend and pleased that she had not driven him away. She knew she was not ready yet for a more committed relationship and she still wanted to keep her old defenses available.

The last session I had with Sylvia was at the end of November. It was a bad year for sickness. A viral pneumonia of a particularly virulent strain swept through the city. Sylvia became ill with a fever and was hospitalized. I went to the intensive care unit to see her. She had a vent in her throat, was receiving oxygen, and could not speak. Her large golden brown eyes looked directly into mine. I spoke to her. I don't recall exactly what I said—words of comfort I believe. I told her I would come again. On my way out, I met her pulmonologist and asked how he thought Sylvia was doing. He had been a colleague and friend for years. He said, "I don't think she's going to make it."

I was shocked. It was hard to believe that this woman who had fought so hard to understand and change herself was going to die at the point where becoming a self-actualized person was finally in her grasp.

I remember standing in the corridor and wondering if there was any value to the whole therapy with her. That night Sylvia died. I called her mother to say whatever one says at these times. Her mother thanked me. Although she sounded somewhat dispassionate, I was sure she was grieving. I know I was.

—B. Shulman

References

American Psychiatric Association. (1994). *Diagnostic and statistical manual of mental disorders* (4th ed.). Washington, DC: Author.

Kolb, L. C. (1982). *Modern clinical psychiatry* (10th ed.). Philadelphia: W. B. Saunders.

Stone, A. 'Requiem' revisited. *Psychiatric times*, Oct, 1997. pp. 10–12.

5

A Letter
to Daddy

A Brievele Dem Taten

—*The [Jewish] Forward*

Late one summer Sheri came to see me for psychotherapy. She reported that she had had an incestuous relationship with her father from age six to age thirteen. Now, at thirty-three, unmarried, she found herself obsessing "uncontrollably" about her father and their sexual experiences. She believed that the incest had colored her entire life and that, because of it, she could not make a long-term commitment to one man. A few months previous she had broken an intense yearlong relationship with a man; she blamed her own depressive behavior and "irrational" outbursts of rage and hostility.

Although she had been in treatment for a year with another therapist, she did not "feel helped." When a former patient recommended me, she came. She said her work in an office brought no gratification, but she did not believe herself capable of doing anything else. She lived alone in her studio apartment, enjoyed a few close friends, and did not lack for the attention of men. Her parents were divorced, both remarried; Mother lived in Chicago, Father, out of state. There was a brother in business with Father.

Sheri gave as her reason for coming that she was depressed. She reported "feelings of inferiority," poor sleep, long bouts with diarrhea, and said she had lost ten pounds in the last year. She denied suicidal ideation, but said there were long periods of time during which she isolated herself from social companionship because, she said, "I can't stand myself or anybody else."

Two years earlier, at the urging of a therapy group, she had decided to confront her father about the incest. She and Father met with a therapist, and when they did, Father responded to her accusation by saying he thought she had "forgotten." When she angrily continued, he answered her by saying she had "enjoyed" and "encouraged" the relationship and finally, he became angry himself. They had previously been on outwardly good terms, but their relationship deteriorated to mutual recriminations and eventually to no contact at all. In contrast, Sheri had never before been close to her mother. After the fiasco with Father, she told Mother about the abuse and Mother became supportive and encouraging to Sheri for the first time in her life. She now had a good relationship with Mother and expressed hatred for Father. Brother, who had never been friendly, distanced himself from Sheri even further when she told him about the incest.

I seriously questioned the notion that the proper way to deal with the situation was to angrily confront the perpetrator and expect him to dissolve in guilt. To confront and accuse seemed to be asking for a fight.

My other question had to do with Sheri herself. How was she handling the trauma of her childhood? Although I would never make light of what had happened to her, I believed she need not make a tragedy of the rest of her life. I questioned whether or not Sheri was in the process of making a "career" out of the "incest tragedy." So far, she had managed to upset a great many people. For example, after the confrontation interview Father refused to have anything do to with her. Her brother responded to her letter by saying she was "in the hands of the wrong therapist." The man she had been involved with was treated to violent, stormy scenes during which she accused all men of being "pigs."

All the excitement creation, all the emotional arousal, all the ventilation in groups with other women who shared similar experiences, and the battles with Father, trying to make him accept the responsibility for his behavior, had added up to the creation of a clinical depression. What had this accomplished for her? I believed that matters were worse than they would have been had she not set out to punish Father. Victims who set out to fight always arrange to lose. Once a person has defined herself as a "victim" she *must* lose in order to reinforce her life-style.

Here was the dilemma: On the one hand Father *had* exploited his female child, taken advantage of her desire to please, and, as Sheri said, father's incestuous attention to her had been "the only affection I got in the house." Father's stroking made her feel good when she was a child. But what did she want now? She seemed to want revenge, but her idea of revenge was to have father beg her forgiveness, admit he was a miscreant for doing what he did, accept full responsibility for his gross behavior, feel shame and guilt, and humble himself to Sheri so she could graciously forgive him. Then they would walk hand in hand into the sunset. It was clear she would never get this from the man she was describing as her father. But, I saw no reason she could not get *something*. She *needed* something from her father. And so that very first day I did something perhaps rather startling. I suggested to Sheri that she try to get revenge, but in a "smart" way. Father was rich, so why not manipulate to get all the money she possibly could? Now, she knew he did not part with his money easily and had already accused her of bringing up the incest with an eye to making money out of it, and so I asked her to see a lawyer and find out whether there were any legal steps she could take. The psychological steps used so far had not brought her the revenge she wanted. Perhaps gaining revenge through legal means would help her to feel better about herself.

Sometimes, in the initial interview, I seek to impress new clients, saying or suggesting something novel. I would like them to leave the first interview with something to think about. Occasionally, I will make an interpretation that normally would be offered only after many long, hard months of working through. It doesn't matter whether the interpretation is accepted, only that the client have something to think about. Usually, I am a very interested, intensely alert, and caring listener. But I listen to my feelings as well, and in this case I thought, "This woman needs a new way of looking at an old problem."

First, I referred her to women's services sponsored by the YWCA in Chicago so that she could see a lawyer about any legal steps that might be taken. Then, I told Sheri that there were other ways to get what she wanted from father and that what she might try to do was to *get money as a form of reparation*. She would not get a "confession"; she would not get the satisfaction of having him accept responsibility for his behavior. What was left? Money! Sheri seemed intrigued.

A few weeks later, without any further reference to the subject on my part, Sheri went to see a lawyer recommended by women's services. The lawyer, a woman, told her the statute of limitations had run out. Sheri looked at me strangely and said, "The lawyer said the same thing you did: Why don't I make up with him and try to manipulate him so that I get a lot of money from him?" The congruence between the lawyer's advice and mine must have made an impression on Sheri for she seemed to pay closer attention to me from then on.

The First Months of Therapy

During the first few months of therapy, Sheri became more depressed. For weeks at a time she would go to work, return home, and "veg out" in front of the TV. When she did go out, she would complain that she felt self-conscious and got no enjoyment out of any social contact. The men she dated were never "good enough—they don't change me, make me forget, or erase the black cloud I bring into the relationship."

In sessions she related dreams in which she and her father were engaging in some kind of sexual activity. The dreams took place in the house she lived in as a child, and were full of hurt and anger at Father (in one dream she saw him mangled), but also full of sexual acts that gave her pleasure. She would awaken upon orgasm.

The fact that she felt pleasure was a problem for Sheri. She knew she had enjoyed the sexuality with Father, that she had had orgasms (as had he), and that what he had done to her had "felt very good." We discussed the fact that she was a sexually responsive woman and that this might very well be a result of the continual sexual arousal as a child. When very depressed, Sheri would complain that she felt no sexual longings and "didn't even masturbate." But even during the worst of her depression she would dream about Father, and almost always in her dreams the two of them were engaged in some sexual activity. She was furious with Father, but her dreams revealed what she would never admit: she still wanted him.

By this time, Sheri's depression was so severe I urged her to get a medicine evaluation. During the course of a depression there is a change in many chemical processes as well as a change in the body's natural rhythms—circadian rhythm is disturbed, sleep is fragmented, energy levels are down. A decision to no longer be depressed is a beginning, but it may still take time for the physiological processes to turn around. I was aware of this and therefore thought a trial of antidepressants would be helpful to Sheri. She did see Dr. Shulman; an antidepressant was prescribed and it helped.

She had uncontrollable crying spells, a constant "lump in her chest," and she was talking about suicide. "It would be a relief to be dead," she said, but she promised to call me and go to the hospital if she ever really wanted to die. (She has never called me for any kind of emergency.) She spent many of our therapeutic hours telling me how "stupid, helpless, inept, un-motivated" she was and how she couldn't "help anything or change anything."

This was a hard time for me. Sheri was in a major clinical depression, and experience has taught me that there really is not much I can do except be very supportive and encouraging, make frequent contact, be sympathetic, and perhaps offer a dollop of exploratory therapy. She listened when I talked about psycho-dynamics, but on the whole she was not ready to examine her own dynamics, even though I persisted.

Analysis

It was during this period that I took the time to understand Sheri's life-style by obtaining specific information about her formative years and the family factors that had influenced her personality development, as described in chapter 1. The following is a summary of her family constellation:

> The younger of two and only girl in a family with a dictatorial czar for a father who was not able to relate to the family except as a dictator. Each family member responded to Father's exercise of power in different ways: Mother played the role of an inferior female in order to be less threatening to Father and used techniques that caricature femininity in order to establish her territory. Brother imitated Father and became "junior czar," and he was supported by Mother, who indulged him. Sheri imitated Mother both in outward compliance and in inner resentment. Power over others was the highest value and was achieved by hook or by crook.
>
> Sheri found herself in an inferior position because of her gender, and because the family dynamics did not automatically grant family members a worthwhile place. Sheri discovered that if she submitted to Father, she could be his favorite and thereby achieve some vicarious power.

Analysis of early recollections gives the therapist the opportunity to understand the patients' basic beliefs about themselves and their phenomenological worlds. Recollections also reflect client's values: they tell us what patients find important and meaningful and where clients' central focus is when looking at the world. The individual psychologist is concerned with the client's "private logic" (as opposed to consensual validation), their final fictive goals (what confers significance), their guiding self-ideals (what they strive to be), and the methods they use for striving. Where these beliefs interfere with successful growth, we hope to change them. Eliciting early recollections at different points in therapy can show changes in perceptual outlook.

These are Sheri's early memories from the first few months of therapy:

> *Three years old:* I'm standing up in my crib. Brother's bed is on another wall. I want a doll that I see across the room, and I can't get it. I cry. I feel frustrated. I'm alone in the room.

Two years old: I was crawling around on the floor in the living room. People are there and the TV is going. I'm crawling around, stopping, looking around. Everybody else is watching television. I have a feeling of solitude.

Six years old: First grade. I beat up a neighborhood kid, a boy. He pissed me off, so I grabbed him by the arm and was twirling him around; then I let him go and he bumped his head on a pole. Somebody came and helped him. I stood there feeling very bad, like a criminal. I said to myself, "How could you?"

Five years old: In the house. My parents had gone out of town and were returning. They came in with a dog. I felt real happy. It was exciting and nice to have them come back.

If we interpret the recollections as conveying the meaning Sheri gives to her life, her subjective convictions, we can see her feeling of alienation from others and her frustration. She cannot attain her desired goals; she is not in the mainstream of her social network. Her actions lead to nothing useful. If she asserts herself, she does damage to others and feels like a bad person. The only happy memory is the one in which she passively depends on the behavior of others (her parents came back). In no memory is anyone glad to see her. The summary is as follows:

> I am too small, too hemmed in, to achieve my goals, and there is no one to help me. Surrounded by others, I am still really alone, in my relationship with others, I, at least, want to be the person who acts justly and with consideration so that I can have some positive feelings about myself. I do not get much positive feeling from others.

The reason for this particular construction is therapeutic. Rather than say in the summary that she sees herself as causing hurt to others, we would prefer to use an ego-syntonic interpretation. We use the information that she feels guilty when others are hurt to attribute to her an ideal of acting with consideration for others (even though she often does not). In so doing we tried to show her that we find something positive in her, and hope that this will not only improve rapport, but also oppose her self-deprecation.

Sheri paid close attention during the analysis and agreed with or added to the summary. She cried throughout the whole interview, but when I gave her a copy of what was written, she merely glanced at it and put it away. I took this to mean she was not prepared to deal with the issues raised and that I could expect a long period of depressive tactics. Unhappily, I was right.

Sheri ventilated endlessly about how inferior she felt, how dumb she was, and how socially inferior she could be. After one blind date she assumed that since she had not been vivacious and charming, the man would never want to see her again. She had started taking courses in library science, and whenever she had an exam, I would hear comments such as "I can't concentrate," "I'm dumb," "I'll do what I have done with everything else and never see it through." (In fact, she graduated with a solid B average.) In addition, she often repeated, "I'm too old for any man to want to marry me."

This was accompanied by crying, sighs, reports of anxiety attacks, and obsession with father. She "hated" him, he was a "scumbag," he had "ruined her life," and because of him, she couldn't "get along with anybody, especially men." "I think that everybody is looking at me and can see how sick I am. I obsess about how nervous and uncomfortable I am with every human being on this planet."

I was reluctant to carry on these discussions with Sheri, believing that such an endless recitation of symptoms and character flaws is not only useless but also antitherapeutic. I tried various methods to get Sheri to stop the endless rumination. Once, listening closely, I began to understand something and said, "Sheri, do you feel flawed?" She responded with a deep sigh of relief, as if I finally understood everything she had been trying to tell me for so long. "Yes," she said, "that's exactly how I feel."

Then Sheri told me how horribly ashamed she felt about the incest, and how she had tried for almost twenty years to put it out of her mind. She knew that she "needed" (wanted) her father, and the truth was, she loved him. During her childhood, Mother lavished love and attention on Brother and Mother was so intimidated by Father's tyrannical demands that she often behaved like a simpleton. Sheri described sitting on Father's lap in the living room with a blanket over their lower parts. Mother would also be sitting in the room since they were all ostensibly watching TV. Father would take off Sheri's pants, expose his penis and rock Sheri back and forth, his penis rubbing against her genitals, until they both reached orgasm. Although she was worried that Mother might notice and say something, Mother did and said nothing.

Mothers in incestuous households often use selective perception. It is important for them to filter out information that would result in cognitive dissonance and so they do not register what is happening. Many perceive themselves as helpless and dependent on their male provider. Even if they allow themselves to see the incest, many women have little knowledge of available resources and are frightened of consequences. Children often understand more than they are able to verbalize and recognize the perceived helplessness of the mother and do not often turn to her during the incest period.

It is folly to expect penitence from the father. No man would exploit a child if he had a conscience in the first place. In "recovered memory" cases so much time has passed since the crime that whatever guilt the father did feel has dissipated and the facts rearranged. It is difficult to live with the knowledge of having wronged somebody. Eventually, guilt turns to anger and people begin to feel hostile toward those they have hurt. Seldom do fathers repent, and, if they do admit misbehavior their stance is, "You liked it as much as I did. You asked for it."

And here lies the guilty little secret; the sex feels good. Incest victims seldom discuss this issue since they feel ashamed of the feelings and question themselves over whether they were in some way responsible for the adult's behavior.*

Sometimes incest victims talk about forgiveness. The pope absolved his attacker, but most of us are not able to offer for-

---

*In the past, psychologists blamed the victim and called the prepubescent girl provocative and abnormally seductive.

giveness to those who have grievously injured us. The act of incest is reprehensible, beyond "forgive and forget." Since there is no justification for some behavior, sometimes the therapist has to allow victims to remain angry and unforgiving at their oppressor. It is not necessary to forgive those events that should not be forgiven.

During the early years of Sheri's life there were constant battles in the house—one fight ending with Brother hitting Mother and Mother having him arrested. Mother, most likely deeply unhappy, ran away with another man when Sheri was fifteen. Little wonder that Sheri believed her only salvation lay with Daddy.

There were several years when Sheri did not see or speak to her mother and she clung to her father. They had stopped the sexually explicit behavior when Sheri started to mature and pushed Father away, but Sheri admired her Father, thought he was wonderful, and believed in him and in his ability to keep everything in order. Years later, when the media started to discuss incest openly, she was reluctant to dredge up her memories. She had told no one about her sexual behavior with Father, and always felt that deep within herself she was flawed so deeply that no matter how she looked on the outside, her inside was so rotten that anybody who got too close, especially a man, would notice.

I believed the truth was that Sheri loved Father and still thought of him as a sexually attractive man. She did miss him, she did think about him, and almost all her dreams were about him.

Dreams

We treat dreams as a projection of the client's current concerns as well as current mood. Dreams also have a prospective function and can be understood as a rehearsal for action. Primarily however, the dream is a metaphor, and dreams, like any metaphor, can be interpreted and translated into rational language. They are used clinically to understand and define problem areas, to predict near-future action, and to teach clients to observe and understand their own internal dynamics.

About eight weeks into therapy, Sheri brought in the following dream:

> I was in the bedroom [in her childhood home] getting clothes so I could leave. My father and I were in twin beds. He kept saying, "Good night, Sheri, good night, Sheri." I couldn't turn out the light. I kept thinking there's another light and yet another to turn off. My brother came in and looked around with a "I wonder what's going on" look on his face. I didn't say anything. I just looked at Father and shrugged, "Let him think what he wants to think."

A few nights later, she had a similar dream.

> I was in the same bedroom at our old house. I was going to sleep. It was warm and I was going to take everything off under the covers. Father was there. I was waiting and wondering if he would come over and bother me. Sure enough, he did. Marvin walked in and Father became very careful. I was aroused—that bugs me. I was going to stop him, but I was aroused.

These dreams demonstrate the recurring issues during the first six months of therapy. Sheri was concerned about her ambivalence in wanting father and wanting to get away from him. She mentioned that the lights were on, which, I think, was her way of saying she was going to expose (turn the lights on) the whole affair.

These dreams demonstrate clearly how much Sheri still wanted Father and how angry she was both at herself and at Father because of the way she felt. In each dream she reminded herself about the incest and refueled her unhappiness. In her dreams she told herself, "I would like my father to still be interested in me." She wants her father.

One Year Later

A year went by. Sheri came to see me weekly. Her dreams showed little change, and she still spent considerable time reciting her list of "inferiorities." Although she was still pursuing her studies in library science, designed to help her change jobs, she suffered whenever there was an exam even though she was really handling it quite well. She was dating intermittently but was always critical of the men and believed they were always critical of her, no matter what their behavior.

Slowly, gradually, she began to feel better, and some of the depression lifted. We became friendly, and I found her charming and witty and possessed of a delightful sense of humor. I found I could tease her and enjoyed her company.

We had started taping our sessions because I wanted Sheri to listen to her self-derogation and perhaps hear some of the interpretations I was busy making to no avail. The following excerpt is a good example of our interaction. I try first to show Sheri the fallacies in her logic and then, in a pixieish mood, enjoy having fun with her.

SHERI: Dorothy, everything is so bad, but what I really can't stand is the inconsistency. At least, at one time, my life was consistently. . .

DOROTHY: Black.

SHERI: Black. Bad, and sad too. But now, periodically, I feel better, and I look at things in a very nice frame of mind.

DOROTHY: Does that frighten you?

SHERI: Maybe it does. Because I always blow it. I always replace the good frame with the bad frame.

DOROTHY: Great! I'm encouraged by the fact that you have good times. You sound like you are *dis*couraged by the fact that you have good times.

SHERI: It's not that I'm discouraged by it, but it is discouraging that somehow I decide to shift myself out of it all the time . . .

DOROTHY: Do you really mean "*I* shift myself?" You mean you understand you are doing it to yourself?

SHERI: Well, I'm not really sure. I just know it starts and then it is a ball that just rolls. It's like I said to you before, I shift myself in and out. I sat down and drove myself nuts. All of a sudden it indicated to me that I was stupid. . . . I went crazy for about a half hour. Then I stood up and gave myself a lecture.

DOROTHY: Which consisted of what?

SHERI: If you don't put this shit aside, you are just going to sit here like this the rest of your life. It worked. For the next couple of days I felt good. I had dealt with myself. It was such a wonderful feeling! The next thing I know, I was overeating to the point that I was feeling uncomfortable.

DOROTHY: Why do you think you do it?

SHERI: I don't want to feel good. I don't want to look good.

DOROTHY: Yes, you do. You want to feel good, you want to look good.

SHERI: I do? So why do I pack myself with food for days and days? My appearance is very important to me, and I am very unusual looking. [She is.] When I do something to mar my looks, I am saying, "Look at me, I don't look good."

DOROTHY: Do you think, by chance, that you are caught up in the cultural thing that we are all supposed to be skinny— you are not supposed to indulge yourself, ever?

SHERI: Indulging is one thing, but gorging is another—for five or six days, that's not just rebelling, that's anarchy!

DOROTHY: Sheri, you don't allow yourself the slightest bit of leeway. "I'm not supposed to overeat, ever." "I'm not supposed to make mistakes when I do my homework." "I'm not supposed to . . ." Whatever else you were telling me just now. It seems to me you never stop picking on yourself. You are not very nice to yourself. Is a bubble bath all right? [Sheri shakes her head "no."] A bubble bath is not all right? Why?

SHERI: Bubbles are bad for your vagina. [Laughter.]

DOROTHY: What if the culture decides within the next couple of years that 175 is an appropriate weight for you?

SHERI: I'll know exactly how to get there. [Laughter.]

The above exchange is shortened from one of the tapes, but I use it to demonstrate our interaction in a humorous and playful mood. Sheri complained about various defects in herself—

inconsistency, driving herself "nuts," compulsive overeating, and similar faults. I tried to counteract her self-deprecating behavior by encouraging her to recognize that her self-criticism was exaggerated. When Sheri seemed to see that she created a negative mood in herself, I introduced the question of why she does this. I saw this self-deprecation as a form of resistance. It is an expression of Sheri's "spoiled" self-image and is an example of Horney's "self-contempt" (Horney, 1946).

This kind of behavior is also a form of overdramatization. One might say that, feeling she has little to contribute in a positive way, she finds significance in being so "flawed." This allows her to have a sense of self that conforms to her self-image. She cannot yet accept certain improvements in herself—she doesn't yet feel "whole."

The session was notable for its playfulness, but there was a method to my madness. The playful mood permitted me a considerable amount of interpretation, and also permitted the use of exaggeration and nonsense to drive home a point. I tried to confront Sheri with two important concepts: first, she is excessively self-critical, and second, she had been self-punitive and has the power to change that behavior.

Later in the same session we returned to her feeling that she goes "up and down."

DOROTHY: Let's go back to the beginning of the tape and listen to how you told me that you go up and down instead of always being flat and depressed. You have also told me on occasion, and again just now, that you have control of it.

SHERI: It seems to me that if you have control and you know you do and choose to have a shitty feeling, then you are worse off than if you are unaware.

DOROTHY: You're right. You're not getting better, you're getting worse. Is that your logic?

SHERI: Yes.

DOROTHY: O.K., I agree with you. Would I fight such logic? It's obvious you're right. That means you're getting worse.

Because you have periods when you feel better and periods when you can talk yourself out of it, the logical conclusion is, "I'm getting worse."

SHERI: It doesn't sound as logical as it did before. And I believe this shit. I really believe this shit.

DOROTHY: It's hard for me to believe you really believe.

SHERI: With this you believe I am ready for a group? [I had been trying to persuade Sheri to join my therapy group.] To sit for an hour and a half and be respectful and kind toward other people when I know I'm a total basket case?

DOROTHY: You'll be the only one in the group that will be respectful and kind to the others. Hurry up and come in.

The above illustrates a common unconscious mechanism that can be considered a form of incomplete insight. Sheri admitted that she recognized how her own style of thinking led her to exaggerate difficulties and thus to create anxiety. She recognized that she had some conscious control over her thinking and over the production of her anxiety. Rather than see this as a hopeful sign, she criticized herself for continuing to engage in her habitual behavior even though she had learned that she does not have to. The self-criticism is simply a continuation of her previous behavior and further permitted her to deprecate herself.

Changes

After several months I was interested in evaluating what progress had taken place. Symptom complaints had subsided, but I wanted to know whether there had been a change in psychodynamics, therefore I collected another set of early recollections:

Six years old: At a holiday dinner at aunt and uncle's house. The cousins were playing and having fun. There were balloons on the backs of the chairs. The room was well lit. The whole family sat at the table and we were talking and eating. I felt happy.

Seven years old: My paternal grandmother from Wisconsin was staying at my house. She and I sat on the patio and talked for a long time before we went to sleep. It was pleasant.

Six years old: I grew big pumpkins. Once morning I went out to tend my pumpkins and the biggest one was gone. I was very upset. I went outside and saw my pumpkin had been dropped in the alley. I felt better because if I couldn't have my pumpkin, then the thief shouldn't have it.

The recollections show considerable change in Sheri's social feeling. She is with people and enjoying herself; she belongs. She is no longer crawling around feeling neglected and alone. But, she is still looking for revenge. I was encouraged by the change in the recollections because they showed an increased feeling of belonging.

Resistance

When the therapist begins to challenge the cherished beliefs of the client, he/she "appears as the representative of the human community," and will "call forth the spite that the patient feels against human society" (Dreikurs, 1967, p. 32). This rebelliousness and the client's desire to escape from the interpretations that point to this antagonistic attitude are two important tools of resistance.

When I believed the therapeutic relationship was firmly established, I challenged Sheri often about the constant restatements of her feelings of inferiority, which actually prevented us from moving to other issues. Once or twice, to dramatize my concern, I pretended to fall asleep. Sheri would laugh and continue her recital. I often tried to discuss with her the purpose of this behavior. She would listen politely and continue. I considered this resistance.

One day I spent an entire session discussing the purpose of Sheri's repetitious recital and her obsession with her feelings of inferiority. I offered one possible purpose and asked her to offer another. Between us we compiled a list of possible purposes for such behavior: it reinforced her old beliefs of not belonging with others, it served to impress her and others with her failings so others would not expect too much, it protected her against taking risks, it allowed her to claim special exemption, and it fed her desire for revenge. Neither of us laughed during this interview.

The following week Sheri came in very angry at me. She told me that I had been "irritable," that I had "jumped" on her, that I had "contradicted" her. She asked whether I was going through a "difficult time." I was taken aback but asked her whether she remembered what we had talked about the previous week or had listened to the tape. She had not and did not want to be interrupted. I asked myself, "What had I done?" Had I been unpleasant or irritable? However I had behaved, I didn't think I deserved quite as much flak as I was getting, and I understood her response as resistance to my interpretation of her behavior. I stayed away from any discussion of psychodynamics for several weeks, replying to her attack by suggesting she would have to learn to put up with me since "I, too, am a flawed human being."

On consideration, I understood that Sheri had achieved her purpose; she did not want to discuss or pay attention to her psychodynamics, and I had accommodated her. I had failed to align our goals. My goal was to get Sheri off of the subject of her inferiorities and onto the subject of her psychodynamics. Sheri's goal was to continue her neurotic strategy of deprecating herself, feeding her anger, and maintaining her posture as a "spoiled" person rather than making peace and beginning a more productive existence.

This particular manifestation of resistance to change continued throughout therapy with Sheri. She spent countless amounts of time in therapy telling me about everything she had done wrong and all the ways she could find fault with herself. The following exchange illustrates her obsession with her inferiorities. She had just met a new man, Sonny, and was beginning to feel very attracted to him, but had previous arrangements with a different man for the weekend before our session.

SHERI: We talked this through, Sonny and I. And I said to him, "Look, I made these plans before I met you." And I told him I wasn't really comfortable about it but I was going to make the best of it. I couldn't ruin the vacation of three other people. He wasn't pressing it, but at the same time I felt a little uncomfortable about it.

Everything is going fine, Dorothy, and all of a sudden Sheri decides she feels uncomfortable, she feels weird around these people, she's not part of the group—she's flustered, she's unhappy, she's depressed, she's an egoist. Fuck.

DOROTHY: I've heard this before. You know you don't believe all this stuff.

SHERI: I do when I can't talk myself out of it. I feel like such a nerd. Such a weak, helpless nerd. I can't stand this. I just don't roll along with life. Everything is such a fucking, goddamn big deal for me. Everything.

DOROTHY: Why should you go along with life when you don't believe it is going to be nice to you? Please repeat your list for me. I lost some of it. You're no good because...

SHERI: I'm so fucking neurotic.

DOROTHY: You can be, but you and I may not agree about what is neurotic about you.

SHERI: What is it, then? What am I doing this for? What am I going nuts about?

DOROTHY: I think things are going too well and you really like this new man Sonny and you want to make sure you are neurotic so nothing happens. You're so afraid to make a relationship that might turn into something that you have to make sure you have diarrhea all over it first. You could make a relationship with Sonny, couldn't you? Something good could come out of it, couldn't it?

SHERI: Yeah.

DOROTHY: So what are you going to do to fuck it up? What are you afraid of? Is he going to hurt you?

SHERI: I think he is not going to love me. I'm not good enough. And eventually he is going to find out and he is not going to love me.

DOROTHY: What about telling him you are neurotic? Tell him

when you start to fuck it up, when you begin to have in-feriority feelings. He'll understand.

SHERI: Well, I did mention to him something like, "Don't let me fuck this up, it's really nice." He said to me, "You better not."

He's such a positive person. What the hell would he want with me?

DOROTHY: I'm not going to give you a list of your attributes. Can you give me one reason, one good reason that I'll accept, why he would not want you? A reason I'll accept.

SHERI: I'm crazy.

The Letter

During this period there had been notable changes in Sheri's outward behavior. She reported that she felt much less depressed. She was more active socially and she and Sonny seemed to be falling in love. She had finished the library science course and was actively looking for new employment. And she started a new relationship with her father.

One day Sheri made a comment about sending a letter to father to "milk him for money." I neither encouraged nor discouraged the idea, but I began to think about Sheri's "revenge." I continued to stress that although Father was never to be forgiven, she must not continue to devote her life to her obsession about the incest. I suggested she try to make Father want her to forgive him. This would allow her to feel in a supe-rior position in relation to her father. From this position, I hoped she would feel a sense of self-respect and self-esteem.

I tentatively suggested to Sheri that she write to Father in a completely conciliatory tone, accepting responsibility for the childhood sexual experiences, in order to reduce Father's indig-nation. Sheri was very interested, and over the course of a few weeks we constructed a letter. We chuckled when we wrote it and tried to outdo each other with what we considered outra-geous sentiments. I never pressed Sheri to compose it and, after it was written, never urged her to send it. It read as follows:

Dear Dad,

I've been in therapy a while now and I've had all this time to explore my childhood. I've sorted things out about our relationship when I was a child. One of the things I realize is that I must assume some of the responsibility for what happened between us.

I understand what I did as a child. I idolized you as the most wonderful daddy a little girl could have. To me you were the epitome of what a man should be—very masculine, strong, forceful, handsome, yet sensitive. To this day it's what I look for in a man. I miss my daddy as part of my life. Not having you in my life has left me very empty.

I don't know if it will ever be possible to be as close as we once were. But perhaps there is some way for you to be some part of my life again. I'm lonely without my daddy. I've been hurting for years because you haven't been with me and don't seem to love me as you did when I was a child. It hurt me not getting letters all these years. I want my daddy.

Your loving daughter,
Sheri

Then Sheri became uninterested in the letter, and it wasn't until many months later that she asked me for it. Father's Day was coming and she wanted to send her father the letter. I gave her the letter and chose not to discuss it further.

What was the reasoning, the purpose behind the letter? First, the letter was a trick, a ploy. Second, the letter could reestablish the relationship, but this time Sheri would be the one in the cat-bird seat. This could change her perception of the relationship. Third, where she used to feel powerless, she could now feel empowered and perhaps be able to stop feeling like a suffering victim.

Father called and said he was "thrilled" with the letter. He blamed the previous therapist for the "division" between them. They talked for a long time and planned a visit (which he paid for). She told him about Sonny and father said, "I want you to have a gigantic wedding, and I'll pay for it, and I won't even have to be there." We both understood this to mean that father believed that once she married, he could believe that he had not inflicted any permanent injury on her, that she had been "cured"—and he would be relieved of guilt.

The visit with father went well and when Sheri returned she seemed to be very pleased about the renewed relationship. She now had the feeling that she was in charge, that she was the one in control and this helped her to feel empowered.

Bankruptcy

Sheri had been seeing Sonny for several months and they were discussing the possibility of marriage. Concerned that she might impose her "neurotic shtick" into the relationship I cautioned her. She agreed to watch herself closely, but continued to tell me about her feelings of inferiority. This time, when discussing the possible purposes of the continuation of these feelings we concluded that her feelings of inferiority were a form of "insurance" against disappointment.

The following week she walked in crying. She had been at dinner at Sonny's parents' home and believed she had not acquitted herself well. After she presented a recitation of "what I did wrong at my boyfriend's house," the following exchange took place:

DOROTHY: Do you think those people are so critical?

SHERI: I think everybody is critical. Everybody is looking at me, and thinking that there's something wrong with me and everybody can see that I'm flawed.

DOROTHY: I want to make an interpretation to you, but it is very unpleasant and I don't think you can take it. [Trying to forestall resistance.]

SHERI: Yes, I can. Go ahead. Go on!

DOROTHY: OK. You seem to think everybody is looking at you and thinking about you and talking about you. It's as if people have nothing else to do but stare at you.

SHERI: [Laughs] I like myself best when I'm at ease and comfortable and don't care what anybody thinks of me— but I can't be like that.

I took exception to Sheri's use of the word *can't*: I tried to help her see that the appropriate word was *won't,* and until she was ready to say "I won't" instead of "I can't," she was not accepting the responsibility for her own behavior. At this point I used my strongest maneuver: I declared bankruptcy. I told Sheri that I had tried everything I knew to help her, that although she had made progress and was doing very well, apparently she didn't share my opinion. I said that I did not know how to help her get rid of her bad feelings, that since she was still claiming inferiority, she must have good reason for continuing her behavior, but that I had exhausted all possibilities and could not think of anything else to do that might be useful to her. I told her I would continue to see her, but was not so sure I could be of any help until she was willing to accept the responsibility for her own feelings and truly understood that she manufactured her oppressive thinking and could (as she had many times in the past) stop herself as well as start herself.

Sheri seemed to be struck dumb and paid close attention. I went back to the original discussion of how she believed people responded to her in social situations.

DOROTHY: Sheri, you seem to be asking for special consider-
     ation. Why do you think you do that Sheri?
SHERI: Because I had such a weird childhood? [A question.]
DOROTHY: What would you like people to do to make you
     feel better? How do you want people to behave in order for
     you to feel that you're all right? Maybe Sonny's mother
     should have said, "Welcome to my house, Sheri. You're the
     most gorgeous, charming woman my son has ever brought
     home. Thank you so much for coming here."

Sheri laughed at the absurdity and said, *"I feel naked without the incest excuse."* The session ended with the following exchange:

DOROTHY: So, the way I see it, you make some very specific
     demands on people when you meet them. One is, "I want

special consideration because of what happened to me
when I was eight years old." And the second statement you
make to the world, and especially to me, is "I won't change
unless my mother and father are different when I was eight
years old."

SHERI: I need an excuse for my behavior.

In the next session Sheri spontaneously brought in some new
early memories that showed further change.

Seven years old: In the classroom. Teacher was talking about
some seeds the class had planted in paper cups. I felt nervous
about it because I hadn't been there when they were planted.
I started to poke the boy in front of me. He turned around
and we started laughing. Teacher got upset and yelled at us.
I felt foolish. Everybody knew I was doing something I
wasn't supposed to.

Seven years old: Father, Mother and I, were in the den. "The
Stripper" (a record) was playing on the record player. I was
parading around and dancing, pretending to strip. Father
was laughing and Mother was chuckling. I liked the attention. I knew he got a kick out of it.

Seven years old: The painter came to our house. I was in love
with him. I hung around him and I talked to him and he
was nice to me. I started to think he really liked me. Then
he finished and left and said, "Goodbye, it was nice knowing
you." I cried when he left. It was as if he had done something to me personally.

The newly evoked memories show that Sheri had heard my
interpretation of the previous session. In the first memory she
seems to be saying, "My therapist knows what I'm doing." She
had been making mischief, and she knew it, at least on an unconscious level. In the next two recollections Sheri is dealing with
her own sexuality. She wants men to be attracted to her and is
happy when they applaud and hurt when it doesn't happen. She
makes it clear she is attracted to men and wants them to like her,

and, best of all, she takes the responsibility for her own behavior. She is no longer playing the role of victim. She has changed her self-perception.

Summary

The case described is that of a thirty-three–year–old single woman who suffered from symptoms of a dysthymic disorder (DSM-IV, p. 169). The main explanation she gave for her distress was an incestuous relationship with her father, which had left her "flawed." During the course of treatment she was able to put the constant obsession with the incest behind her, train herself for a new job, discover that she had more control over her thoughts and moods than she realized, reduce her self-sabotaging behavior, and come out of her depression.

After a number of sessions spent listening to ventilation and complaint, I became increasingly active. I gave Sheri consider-able attention and caring [sincere]. With the use of humor, irony, and conspiratorial assistance in writing the letter, the incessant complaints finally stopped.

My therapeutic style is active, directive, confronting, and intrusive. I offer clarification, interpretation, guidance, and support. Through months of therapy there were only two weeks of resistance and I always felt our relationship to be strongly positive. And when she did accuse me of being unkind, I admitted to being a "flawed" person and continued my support and encouragement.

First, I allied myself firmly with Sheri. Then, acting as an ally, I began to interpret the unconscious plans and convictions that lay behind her behavior. My main endeavor at all times was to lead Sheri to examine her own behavior and choose alternatives. The process of encouragement requires not a neutral but a friendly stance on the part of the therapist, and I sincerely believed that Sheri could find a better meaning to her life.

Mistaken perceptions were brought into the open for exami-nation. Their sources were identified in the early childhood situation, and current troublesome behaviors were interpreted both as a relic of past learning and as having a current safe-guarding value. These behaviors helped Sheri defend against loss of self-esteem and avoid anticipated failures.

One of the ways in which we evaluate clients is to watch their psychological movement. Sheri had used depressive and anxiety-provoking cognitions to nurse her wounds instead of getting on with her life. She had created the self-image of a flawed/abused person who was bad and to whom bad things had been done. The change in the psychodynamics saw Sheri move from being a "helpless, innocent victim" to becoming a caring, responsible human being.

Epilogue

Sheri has read this paper and wants to see it published. There is no depression. She has a friendly relationship with Father and looks forward to his future generosity. Although she has not forgiven him, she no longer spends her time feeling abused. She half-believes that she is not "flawed." She and Sonny will be married soon, and her trepidation is no more than that of any other bride-to-be.

—D. Peven

Note

"A Letter to Daddy" is based on the following:
Peven, D. and B. Shulman. 1986. "Adlerian psychotherapy." In I. Kutash and A. Wolf (Eds.). *Psychotherapist's* (pp. 101–123). San Francisco: Josey-Bass.

References

American Psychiatric Association. (1994). *Diagnostic and statistical manual of mental disorders* (4th ed.). Washington, DC: Author.
Dreikurs, R. (1967). *Psychodynamics, psychotherapy and counseling*. Chicago: Alfred Adler Institute.
Horney, K. (1946). *Our inner conflicts*. New York: W.W. Norton & Co.

6

"Are You Lookin' at Me?"

"Are You Lookin' at Me?"
— Travis Bickle in Martin Scorsese's
Taxi Driver, 1976

Mike was thirty-one years old when he first came to see me. He had asked his family doctor to refer him to a psychiatrist because he had "problems" and because he had felt, since early childhood, that there was "something wrong" with him. Among other anxious thoughts he was worried that he might be homosexual. He offered two reasons for this fear. One was that he had never had a girlfriend because he was too bashful to approach girls, and the other was that he had a very scanty blonde beard and almost no body hair. Because he often felt rage at innocent strangers who were walking by him in the street, he thought that he might do something to harm someone. Sometimes he thought he should go to the local state hospital and ask to be admitted because he thought he was a danger to others.

He believed that he was unattractive and awkward and that others could recognize by looking at him that he was not "normal." And he often assumed that people were viewing him scornfully. He would then feel ashamed and angry and fantasize scolding and hitting them.

It was painful for him to come to the downtown office because the people in the street were better dressed than he was and he thought others would know that he "didn't belong there." He avoided eating in restaurants; he was afraid he would do something gauche and shame himself in front of other diners. He was attracted to females, but never approached them. He did not feel he was good enough for any "sensible" woman to have a relationship with him.

Mike feared that he could not be helped, but he desperately wanted to change the way he felt and behaved. He wanted to be able to talk to people without being uncomfortable, to go into restaurants and other public places, to stop being angry and ashamed of himself all the time.

Mike had seen a therapist on one occasion only about two years earlier. He had told his story to the therapist who listened sympathetically but had made one remark that offended Mike and Mike had never wanted to see him again. When he had described his fear of being homosexual to the therapist, the doctor, no doubt wanting to be sympathetic and encouraging, had said, "Being homosexual isn't the worst thing in the world." Mike reported that he felt instant revulsion. He said to me, "He thought it was OK for me to be homosexual. I couldn't wait to get out of there."

He did not want to be what he thought he was. His self-image was abhorrent to him. It was easy to recognize that this negative self-image was an important part of Mike's problem; but it was also important to note that Mike had an idealized image of how he wanted to be; he did not want to make peace with what he was. His goal was to free himself of his impediments or, failing to do so, have himself put away so he could do no harm. The trait he could like most in himself was his desire not to do bad things. This was the wish and intention that needed to be validated by the therapist.

Mike had another problem that was very embarrassing and which confirmed for him that he was of inferior material. He was a bedwetter. All his life he had wet the bed several times a week. Only his close family knew. He washed his own bed sheets and tried to keep himself clean and presentable. Medical examination had always found no physical reason for the bed-wetting. He tried medication one time, but the first dose made him feel dizzy and he was afraid to take more. He therefore avoided staying at anyone else's house or taking trips.

Current Life Situation

Mike lived in a two-bedroom flat with his father and a younger brother. Mother had died several years earlier of a congenital heart condition. In the upstairs apartment lived Mother's widowed sister who had no children of her own. Mike's relationships with members of his family were cordial. He loved his aunt (upstairs) and one uncle who was a hard-working construction foreman, and he admired his younger brother who was outgoing and popular.

Mike worked as a cabinetmaker at a shop owned by a family friend. Relations on the job were not cordial. The shop opened at 7 A.M., but Mike never felt able to rise that early. He made an arrangement with the foreman that he would come later and work later and thus put in the required number of working hours. He considered this behavior slothful and self-indulgent and kept planning to arrive at work earlier. The other operators on the floor would speak to each other and joke but usually ignored Mike who did not feel comfortable with them. But if Mike greeted them pleasantly, they always responded in a friendly way. Mike believed that he was slower than they were and that they secretly tended to look down on him.

Social activities were limited to his family—aunts, uncles, and cousins with whom he felt comfortable. Mike went to weddings, confirmations, family gatherings, and holiday meals, but he was shy and said little. Yet, he went and was polite to everybody.

Past History

The first born in his family, Mike reported that he had never felt close to his mother. He recalled her as having a bad temper and always being unhappy. It seemed she had spent some time in a psychiatric hospital. One time, while ironing, she had been annoyed by Mike's behavior and threw the iron at him, striking him on the side of the head. Mike was about ten years old at the time. After that, he said he avoided his mother as much as he could. He felt closest to his aunt who used to take him with her when she went shopping, and he had an early memory from age eight when his aunt took him to a toy store for his birthday and told him he could have anything he wanted. His response was to feel embarrassed by his aunt's generosity. He said he felt undeserving and deliberately picked out something unimportant and inexpensive so that she would not have to spend much money on him. Nevertheless, he was grateful to her for wanting to buy him a present.

He had been somewhat in awe of his father and kept distance from him, but began to feel closer after Mother died and he saw how much his father grieved. The one person he could talk to most openly was an uncle (the construction worker) who saw him occasionally and would ask Mike personal questions in a friendly way. Uncle was sympathetic and told Mike that he had some problems of his own with anxiety.

Mike recalled his school days with distaste. His grades were poor, he was a poor reader, he had no lasting friendships, and he was a poor athlete and slow learner. However, he did not misbehave and managed to graduate from high school near the bottom of his class. Mike thought of himself as being an inferior, unworthy person, unintelligent and incompetent.

The first time Mike began to feel better about himself was when he took an after school job in a packing facility. He discovered that he could work as hard as his coworkers and accomplish as much. This led to feelings of accomplishment and he began to enjoy going to work more than going to school where learning was so difficult.

The job experience encouraged him to try to be successful in the army, so he volunteered and concealed his bed-wetting until he actually arrived at training camp. He summoned up his courage, went to his sergeant, and explained his problem (which would ordinarily lead to discharge from the service) and told the sergeant that he would get up early every morning and wash his own soiled bed linen, but wanted to remain in the army. The sergeant appreciated this and accepted Mike's proposition. Thus,

Mike spent two rather happy years in the army with his secret protected. He completed his tour of duty without incident and received an honorable discharge.

It was during military service that Mike had his one and only sexual experience. He went with some other soldiers to a house of prostitution. The lady told him he did well, but he thought of it only as an accomplishment rather than a pleasure: he had wanted to discover if he would be able to function. When he realized that he was potent and could perform normally, he was satisfied and did not pursue further sexual contact.

Psychodynamics

All of Mike's early childhood recollections were of personal failure and self-doubt, or of hostile interactions between people: his mother's anger, his own lack of worth, rejection by his classmates, and young boys being cruel to one another.

Mike was the older of two boys; a firstborn whose early experiences (rejection by a mentally ill mother, learning disorder in school) led him to feel inferior to others. He saw himself as either unloved or unworthy of love. This harsh judgment of himself probably served a useful strategy as compensation for his inferiority feelings. That is, he was his own most severe critic. He did not believe he could attain the same status as others in the competitive masculine world.

Mike saw masculine relationships as basically competitive. He measured himself against the men he knew and decided he was of low caste. He thought other men were more intelligent, physically stronger, had more body hair, made more money, drove better cars, had pretty girlfriends, and so on. On the other hand, Mike could also become very critical of people who seemed to be deficient in some capacity. He would become very angry if he saw people inappropriately dressed, talking too loud in public places or demonstrating otherwise unpleasant social behavior. This was sometimes carried to an extreme: when he saw a blind man walking along the sidewalk tapping his cane on the ground, he thought, "That person is offensive to other people. He shouldn't be out on the street."

To place Mike's dynamics in the template we find useful, we would state the following in the first person. This is how Mike sees himself in the world:

> I am a male who is inferior and of lesser worth (self-image).
>
> Life demands certain attributes and performance from a man and I can't make the grade. The world will judge me as unworthy.
>
> However, I know my faults better than anyone else.

Mike is a good example of several important theoretical concepts: the effect of the inferiority feeling and its source in both physical and psychological factors; the compensatory striving for some form of worth, significance or superiority; and the depreciation tendency as a compensatory device (elevating oneself by depreciating others).

Mike sees himself as "first worst"; that is, nobody has to tell him how dumb and incompetent he is, he already knows. Furthermore, he would like others to know, "You're not so hot yourself." This is what elevates his self-esteem and gives him a feeling of superiority (his compensation). Inferiority feelings and their compensations usually are found linked in this way. If one feels unsuited to one area of life, one can look for another more congenial area in which to thrive. When options exist, one can choose in which area one will strive and which area one will let go. Such choices, often made early in life, influence later interests and pursuits. This is, of course, a constructivist theory. It also requires a motivational element. Compensatory behavior is goal-directed behavior; but compensation and goal are chosen options. It is as if the individual chooses a role and acts it out in the scenes that life events present.

Psychotherapy

A dynamic formulation of a case does not always tell us how the psychotherapy should begin. The contact with the client usually moves naturally from assessment to treatment if the therapist pays close attention to the client's complaints (the reason for seeking help). Mike's complaint was that he was inferior and inadequate, and therefore unhappy and unacceptable to others, confined to the margins of life rather than its center. He was uncomfortable in social situations, less masculine than other males, less competent as a worker, and a bed wetter. These complaints point logically to an assortment of goals that will begin to fashion the therapy. The most obvious part of Mike's problem is a mistaken perception: He exaggerates his deficiencies; they overly discourage him. Also, he makes a mistaken connection between body hair and sexual orientation.*

A second issue is the social phobia behavior. It would be beneficial and important for Mike to learn to be at ease in ordinary social situations. This would require a change in behavior, as well as a different perception of self and others. Third, enuresis in adults without physical reason may be associated with developmental problems, such as a motor learning disability, but can usually be outgrown by the time the person reaches adulthood. A fourth goal would address other complaints Mike had about himself; e.g., he could never rise early enough to get to work on time and he could not read books. I discussed these goals with Mike in an informal way because I felt that a formal statement of goals would be frightening for him. I began by suggesting that we talk about all these problems and see what we could do.

Validation

As I have previously mentioned, Mike had seen another therapist to whom he had expressed his fear that he was homosexual. The therapist, no doubt wanting to be encouraging, suggested that homosexuality was not the worst thing in the world. I remembered that Mike suffered from the fear that he was gay, not from being gay or of being afraid of what others might think or say. To reassure him that it was all right to be gay neither helped him calm his fear nor understand it.

---

*Sparse body hair is fairly common, and is not a sign of impaired masculinity.

If a person is convinced of his inferiority, convincing him otherwise requires considerable proof before it can be believed. At first, it would seem to Mike as if the therapist does not understand him or how inferior he is. It is hard to trust a therapist who does not understand one. Therefore, it seemed to me that first I had to validate Mike's self-image. I had to show that I understood that he considered himself inferior, different, deviant, and would try to help him become more normal. This validation allowed us to align our goals so that we could collaborate.

In working with discouraged clients, it is sometimes useful to start with a task that will be relatively easy to accomplish—in order to foster an encouraging "success experience." Mike came to see me at two-week intervals, when he would tell me about what had happened to him in the interim, voice his complaints, and talk about his inadequacies or the rudeness and insensitivity of others. "Working hard" was a form of behavior he used and so we worked on several goals simultaneously. By working hard he displayed his good intentions and hoped to win some appreciation.

Encouragement

I saw no purpose in interpreting the enuresis and the reading inhibition in a dynamic way and approached these symptoms as learning problems. Both reading and bladder control have to be learned by the child (I explained to Mike) and I would help him learn to do it. I instructed him to use a book that told a story and was easy to read, and to read no more than one page a day, in the evening, before he went to bed. I also instructed him to restrict his fluid intake after 8 P.M. and to keep a daily record of the bed-wetting. Every time I saw him I would ask him about each problem and would duly record it in his chart. I explained to him that gradually the enuresis would decrease and the ability to read would improve. I was reasonably sure that the explicit suggestion and implicit anticipation would gradually have an effect on the behavior. I was right.

Mike never became an avid reader, but became able to read a two-hundred page book in a few weeks and was able to enjoy the stories. As we kept a record of the enuresis, it gradually decreased from three times a week to less than once a month. When Mike had been dry for six weeks, he decided that he was no longer a bed wetter.

These two examples can be thought of as behavior therapy rather than psychotherapy. They are good examples of how therapeutic relationships, once established, can facilitate therapeutic change. What changes in the client is the perception of adequacy/inadequacy. Mike now began to feel able to do things he had not done before. This type of success encourages the client to pursue further goals.

One recognizes immediately that this is not dynamic psychotherapy. The therapeutic relationship at this point is one of a teacher and student. I was telling Mike how to perform a task, giving him homework, and instructing him to anticipate positive results and stay task focused. This, of course, is behavior therapy. But it also created a relationship between Mike and myself in which I could become an authority he could trust. Once he could trust me, he could hear what I was saying. Since I limited our universe of discourse to these simple tasks, I could say many things to Mike in the nature of a running commentary. I could tell him that his social anxiety started in childhood. I could tell him he should have had special tutoring in school. I could explain how enuresis can be overcome by reducing fluid intake, that people like to hear someone say "hello" and smile at them; that he should show his pleasant smile more frequently. I could attribute positive traits to him. He was kind to his aunt, he was unselfish, he was always polite, he seemed to catch on to things quickly, and he was a hard worker. I was, of course, always "positive," and never agreed with him when he told me how inferior he was.

Improving relationships with fellow workers seemed a harder goal to reach. When Mike told me about the other workers I would say to him that he seemed to feel very uncomfortable around them, but that he would really like to get along with them. Mike accepted this attribution and agreed. I began to talk to him about relationships in general. I reviewed with Mike his daily interactions at work. Mike behaved as if he expected hostility and disapproval from others. He had no social relationships with fellow workers, rarely spoke to them, and when he did, was blunt and curt. Mike believed that the other workers were faster than he and more skilled (which may have been true).

I spoke in generalities about relationships, rather than directing Mike about what to do. I spoke about cordial greetings, the value of smiling, the purpose of small talk, the uses of humor, and friendly versus hostile signals, and Mike listened carefully. He then began to report how he deliberately tried to change his behavior and how pleased he was that his changed behaviors led to good results. He was able to engage in friendly badinage, to feel compassion for a fellow worker whose wife was sick, and found that he was not so critical as he had been, nor did he feel so inferior to others. He began to rise earlier in the morning and came to work at 9 A.M. instead of 11 A.M. (even though the plant opened at 7 A.M.)

Occasionally, Mike would admit that he had made improvements in his behavior, but he still had many complaints about himself.

Dynamic Interpretations

From time to time, I would be able to interpret psychodynamics to Mike in a useful way. On one occasion Mike was reporting a symptom that frightened him. The thought would enter his mind of picking up a table knife and stabbing the aunt whom he loved. The thought would occur when he was eating dinner at his aunt's table (she frequently invited him). He told me this with an editorial comment, "The only person who's really nice to me and look what I'm thinking about doing to her ..."

At first glance, such a thought might be seen as a sign of covert hostility toward the aunt. Such would *not* be the interpretation according to a dynamic theory that would ask, "What is the purpose of having such a thought?"

One way of discerning such a purpose is to examine the outcome of the thought. What happens after Mike has the thought? I asked this question and he answered that it made him feel very uncomfortable and he would try to finish his meal quickly and leave his aunt's apartment. He would then be angry with himself and feel ashamed and worry that his aunt would somehow guess what he was thinking.

I made the interpretation stepwise, using further questions:

DR. S.: If having the thought leads you to run away from your aunt, does that mean you can't sit and talk and have a normal conversation with her? You say she is kind and loving and you want to be a help to her, but does it make you uncomfortable to just sit and talk? Is it easier for you to keep a distance from people?

These questions led Mike to admit that "sitting and talking" had always been hard for him. He was always afraid he would say something wrong. It was the reason he had cultivated a gruff exterior at work, discouraging friendly conversation.

We continued:

DR. S: Could it be that since you expect that once people really get to know you, they will reject you, it's better not to let them get to know you too well?

MIKE: I think you're right, but why do I think about stabbing my aunt with the table knife?

DR. S: Have you ever had the thought about stabbing anybody else?

MIKE: I've thought about beating some people up, but I was angry at them. I'm not angry at my aunt, I don't want to hurt her.

DR. S: Maybe because you really do love your aunt, you especially wouldn't want her to know you too well. The result of the thought is that *you stay away from her*. You keep your distance, you hide yourself from her.

When Adler described neurotic symptoms and forms of movement in the psychosocial field he said that "distance-keeping" was "safeguarding behavior," the avoidance of undesired or threatening contact (Ansbacher & Ansbacher, 1956). It seems fairly obvious that social phobia can be interpreted as distance-seeking behavior. And Mike's formal diagnosis *was* social phobia (social anxiety disorder) (DSM-IV, p. 205).

As mentioned above, Mike went to family affairs, but said little and sat on the margins. In his conversation with his brother and father, Mike followed the masculine pattern of conversing to exchange information, but, with the kind aunt, who would ask him questions about himself, Mike would become uncomfortable in order to seek distance. The thought of stabbing his aunt was well suited to its unconscious purpose—to keep a distance from the loving aunt. Nobody likes to be rejected, and we all have different ways of dealing with rejection, but we don't all develop neurotic symptoms.

Reductio ad Absurdum

Mike half-accepted my interpretation of the symptom, but the thought of stabbing his aunt continued and began to have an obsessive quality. Becoming more open and sharing feelings with his aunt was still too threatening for him. At this point I tried something else.

Adlerian theory recognizes that if one struggles against an obsessive thought (as opposed to dismissing it) one actually heightens and dramatizes the thought or fantasy. Dispelling the obsessive thought is easier if one can downplay its importance. I instructed Mike to visualize the scene in which he stabs his aunt, but to imagine that he picks up the napkin from the table instead of the knife and stabs his aunt with the napkin. I said, "The next time you have dinner with her, think about stabbing her with the napkin." Mike was thoughtful and offered to try. The next session he said, "I tried to think about stabbing my aunt with the napkin, but it seemed silly, so I just forgot about the whole thing." From then on, he reported no more obsessive thoughts about stabbing his aunt.

However, the issue of distance keeping was not resolved. He could joke more easily with fellow workers, but still ate lunch alone. He loved his aunt, but was uncomfortable when she asked the kind of personal questions a loving aunt might ask. I considered the possibility that his early relationship with his psychotic mother may have lacked intimacy or affect attachment. In a discursive way, I began to investigate Mike's relationship to his aunt. I would ask, "How is your aunt? Did you have dinner with her this week? How old is she now? Do you help her with anything?" and gradually began to ask questions like, "Do you ask her about her health? Do you ever buy her a present? Do you send her a birthday card?"

Mike was taken aback. He had never thought about doing such things since it hadn't been done in his family. I asked if the aunt might be pleased if he showed his fondness for her. He was excited by the idea and spent the next few weeks agonizing over what the message on the card should say. When he asked me for help I asked him to describe his aunt in detail and tell me what he liked most about her.

Conversations of this type were new to Mike. He soon found a card that expressed his feelings (it was quite tasteful) and gave it to her without waiting for a birthday. Aunt was pleased and told the whole family about "Mike's card." Mike felt quite pleased with himself that he was able to make such a good impression by sending a card. I could then make further general comments that people liked being noticed and appreciated and added, in an offhand way, that Mike seemed to be developing some charm, then hastily added, "But it's too soon to tell."

The Therapeutic Relationship

The particular kind of relationship in this therapy was like that between an accepting an encouraging authority and a student. Tutoring might be a more apt word for this relationship. The unconscious dynamics of Mike's behavior were easy for the therapist to see, but it was not really necessary to interpret or expose these dynamics. What was necessary was for Mike to discover that he was looking at himself the wrong way. The childhood experiences that led to his low self-esteem were quite apparent to him. What he did not see was that his self-image was a mistake. Thus, *teaching* Mike a different way of looking at himself was an appropriate therapeutic approach.

Transference issues did not get in the way. In fact, his transference to me was helpful to him. It is possible that Mike thought I would look down on him, but I believe that my act of taking his complaints seriously and my stating that he was obviously working hard at therapy allowed him to see me as validating and accepting him.

As a result, Mike never showed any significant resistance to what I was saying. He accepted me as an authority on human behavior—he saw me as teaching him how to change and each small victory was evidence to him that he was changing. Liking and trusting his father, it was easy for him to trust me.

This type of therapy is highly directive in fact, but is experienced not as a command to do something but as a shared experiment. I would give specific directions on how to do something (e.g., "Don't read more than one page a night") and be quite certain that Mike would soon find himself reading more than one page and so informing me. I would then show that I was impressed with the speed of his learning, and what started out with a "Do such and such . . ." statement from me would end up with an "I was able to do more than you thought" response from him. I was thus teacher and ally.

Change

Mike's symptoms gradually decreased. He started to eat lunch with his fellow workers and could discuss mundane matters with them. He seldom wet the bed. He arrived at work earlier. He could walk the streets with less discomfort. He could shop in a store and stand in line at the bank without feeling that everyone was looking at him. But he still felt alone and too bashful to seek female company.

A Window of Opportunity

During the course of any psychotherapy, there may occur life events that provide an opportunity for the therapist to offer some useful and important information to the client; information that will provide an insight, correct a mistake, foster a change. One such incident opened the way to a significant change in Mike's life.

Mike owned a dog. He usually walked the dog every evening in the alley at the back of his house. On the other side of the alley, a new family had recently moved in. They also had a dog, which was walked every evening by the daughter of that family, a young woman in her early twenties.

They noticed each other. She smiled as they passed each other and he politely said hello. Although Mike would have kept walking, his dog had other ideas. His dog, a male, approached the other dog (a female) and the two engaged in the sniffing activities that allowed them to get to know each other better. Mike was very embarrassed, pulled his dog away and continued walking.

When he discussed it with me, he said, "I felt like smashing him on the head, killing him. I felt my face turning red. I didn't know what to say and I got away from there as soon as I could. I was so ashamed of the way he acted. I don't even know if I could say 'Hello' the next time I see her!"

This gave me the opportunity to intervene in Mike's customary misperceptions of what was really going on in a social situation. For Mike, every social contact was a measure of social status; every interaction carried the risk that he would make a faux pas and be humiliated. So I said to him: "But, Mike, that's the way dogs are supposed to behave."

This caught his attention and puzzled him (which was my intent). I then explained normal canine behavior, stating that his dog was being courteous and friendly by sniffing the other. Mike was both surprised and pleased, especially when I translated the behavior to human interaction and talked about how to be friendly and polite at the same time; how one's posture and speech sent friendly or unfriendly signals and how to read the signals of others.

Rather than assuming that others were scorning him Mike began to watch others, He found people more friendly than he had expected and understood that he himself could consciously and deliberately send out "friendly" signals to elicit a positive response. He was delighted, but cautious.

He began to experiment with friendly signals in the back alley and starting paying attention to the young lady with the dog. Within a short time she invited him into her house and he was delighted to find he could feel at ease with her family and her.

Within a year they were married.

Commentary

Mike had come for help with his problems, which he understood as unhappiness with perceived deficiencies in himself. The picture he presented allowed us to match him with the DSM categories of social phobia and enuresis. But what Mike wanted was to be able to live in a world that seemed unfriendly, populated by beings to whom he could not measure up. In the language of Individual Psychology, Mike had intense feelings of inferiority and was trying to preserve what place he had by avoiding some situations, aggressively defending himself from others, and even finding occasional compensation by being able to feel secretly better than those whose mistakes and missteps were more obvious.

The symptoms themselves (bed-wetting and social discomfort) match his secret shame and feeling of alienation: his unworthiness and his social incompetence.

The main "mistake" he was making was in his biased image of himself. He found many reasons to consider himself inferior and developed a "heightened awareness" of his inferiorities— e.g. his beard was too scanty, he did not rise early enough, he didn't read books, and so on.

The main direction of therapy (after making clear what the mistakes were) was in the direction of collecting evidence that he was *not* inferior, was *not* much different than others, had unfortunately not been well mothered, and thus had not developed a positive sense of self.

As his therapist, I was consistently encouraging and satisfied with very small steps forward. What I would stress was what he was accomplishing. When he became able to take his girlfriend to a fine restaurant, he reported, "I didn't mind people looking at me, because I was with a pretty girl and I was dressed up. I looked as good as anybody in the room."

This case is a good example of the dynamics of social phobia and persistence of enuresis (without organic cause) into adult life. Mike's "neurosis"—the arrangement of thoughts, feelings, and behaviors that provide for the person a detour around the supposedly insurmountable tasks of life—can be seen as Mike's private arrangement for trying to cope with the world as he saw it.

—B. Shulman

Post Script

One afternoon at the hospital Dr. Shulman and I were called on a consult. Mike was in the hospital for a minor procedure and told the attending doctor that he would like to see Dr. Shulman. We walked into his room and I saw a fair-skinned, plain-looking man in his early thirties. Dr. Shulman introduced me, Mike said "Hello," and I sat down and listened to the conversation. Mike told Dr. Shulman that he would be getting married soon and (apparently again) described how he had met his fiancée. Dr. Shulman asked Mike if he had any "disturbing thoughts." Mike responded:

"Yes, I do. She [his fiancée] has dark hair that she parts down the middle. Sometimes I think I want to take an axe and bring it down right across that part in the center of her head."

I wondered what this man was doing outside of an institution and got ready to leave the room in a hurry. But Dr. Shulman said, "And do you know why you have such thought?"

Mike replied in a flat monotone "Yes. I understand. I have thoughts like that in order to keep distance from my girlfriend."

"Are you going to break up with her?"

"No. I love her and I don't want to hurt her. You taught me why I have thoughts like that."

"Good."

I was stunned. This man was talking about violent behavior and Dr. Shulman had not paid any attention. In fact, Dr. Shulman had ignored the talk about the axe and gone directly to the purpose of the behavior. Mike immediately understood and responded. To me, sitting silently in the corner, Mike sounded like a robot that had a tape running in his head that he turned on when prodded. What had Dr. Shulman wrought?

We left, and Dr. Shulman reassured me that Mike would not ever be violent. But I never forgot Mike and the way he had been "programmed."

—D. Peven

References

American Psychiatric Association. (1994). *Diagnostic and statistical manual of mental disorders* (4th ed.). Washington, DC: Author.

Ansbacher H., & Ansbacher, R. (Eds.), (1956). *The individual psychology of Alfred Adler*. New York: Basic Books.

7

The Replacement

"What Do You Want From Me?"
—Pink Floyd

Christine was twenty-six when her physician referred her to me. She was a well-dressed, pretty, dark-haired girl, recently married to a classmate she had met in law school. At the time she came she was working as an attorney in a large corporate law firm and her husband was working in another department in the same firm.

Christine felt she was in immediate crisis. She had been in analysis for four years and reported that she had had an "intense transference" to her female analyst, Dr. K. During that time she had become obsessively interested in the analyst's personal life. She would find reasons to telephone her in the evening in order to talk to her. After a session, she would linger in the office building to discover what time the analyst left the office. When the analyst retired because of illness and referred Christine to another therapist, Christine felt abandoned and wrote long letters to the analyst describing her unhappiness until the analyst explained she could not continue to answer Christine's letters.

She felt hopeless and angry and reported a variety of symptoms: her appetite was poor, she felt bloated all the time, her sleep was interrupted, and she woke up not knowing where she was. She reported suffering from crying spells, difficulty in concentrating, and a feeling of being overwhelmed by her tasks. She felt "terrified," she "hated" herself, and she felt self-destructive. She had a history of "cutting" and when the analysis was disrupted, she started cutting herself again. Her frequent nightmares frightened her because they were about death, violence, and abandonment. Her fantasies were fearful and sadistic—walking down the street a strange man would attack her. She described herself as "a life-long core of pain."

In law school she had an episode of depression. An older professor, acting as an advisor, had been very kind to her. She knew nothing of his private life and was shocked and grief-stricken when he committed suicide. She was referred to a crisis intervention counselor who told her that her problem was more than simple grief and recommended therapy with a psychoanalyst. She had been seeing the analyst since that time four years ago, but had continued to be depressed.

She thought about suicide, but wouldn't do it because she "didn't want to hurt" her husband or her mother. At the train station she would think about jumping onto the tracks in front of an oncoming train and she kept razor blades hidden in case she decided to cut her wrists.

She worried that nothing she did would be noticed or appreciated. Because she was strongly ambitious and wanted to impress her employers, she worried that she would not be good enough. She worked industriously to write briefs, do research, and present her works for approval to her department chief.

Her husband reacted with compassion to her displays of distress and that was probably an important reason for the success of the marriage. Christine said she loved her husband and recalled how she would often come from a session with the analyst, go to bed, cry, and not want to speak to him, yet he would be understanding and supportive. She said their sexual relationship was just "OK" and she blamed herself for feeling too depressed to want sex.

The Family Tragedy

There had been a tragic event in the family before Christine was born. A sister then two years old had been killed in a drowning accident, for which, apparently, the mother blamed herself.

Mother became pregnant as soon as possible after the child's death and bore Christine about a year later. Christine felt that this had influenced her life in many ways. She believed her role as a "replacement" made her a "special" child and that she had a more unique meaning to her mother than the other children.

> I have to make up for everything. All my life I've absorbed my parents' pain. My role is to absorb the pain and put it inside me. I always carry this core of pain.

Christine had always known about the family tragedy because her mother would talk about it and, jokingly, would call Christine her "replacement." But it was clear that Mother also blamed herself for not watching the older sister more closely and preventing the tragedy. Although Mother never indicated it, Christine began to feel that she was to be the cure for Mother's sorrow. She believed she was not free to be herself, but was obliged to be the daughter her mother wanted and lost.

Such a perception by the child can create a special kind of problem. The child becomes the person responsible for protecting the suffering parent from more distress. If, in order to do this, the child must strive to fulfill all the roles that the dead child would supposedly have accomplished, it places a large burden on the child. Since the dead child is idealized the replacement feels "not good enough" and self-esteem is vulnerable. The desire for achievement and approval becomes more and more pronounced and anything less than perfect is seen as a failure. Criticism, even disagreement, is also seen as personal rejection, and the need for approval is exaggerated.

History

Christine's father was a highly regarded jurist and sat on one of the state courts. Following Father, Christine and her older brother were lawyers. A younger sister was a teacher. She did not feel close to her father because, she said, he seemed authoritarian and critical and showed no special interest in any of his children. Yet she was very close to her mother and described herself as unusually dependent on her. She called her mother several times a day to cry and complain. She was always looking for Mother's comfort, and Mother obliged.

Christine remembered her childhood as full of sadness and fear.

> I was unpopular. I was teased. I was the outcast in Kindergarten. Mother thought I would eventually make friends, but I didn't. I always felt like I was on one side of a fence watching the people on the other side. I had one or two girlfriends, but I never kept them long.

She went on to say that she always felt like an outsider, but she covered up her feelings. She lied, she told made-up stories about the girls and spread rumors. She would try to get the other girls into trouble and was generally mean. She would criticize the girls at school and felt superior because of her grades. But the other girls were more popular, had friends and dates, and seemed happier.

In her academic pursuits she was successful. In college she discovered that men could be attracted to her. The faculty professor who had taken an interest in her allowed her to feel liked for herself and was very supportive. His suicide precipitated her search for help, her entry into counseling, and the start of her analysis with Dr. K., a female psychoanalyst with whom she had a volatile relationship.

She would vent anger at the woman, call her names, and tell her that she was incompetent and uncaring. She made excuses to call her at all hours of the night, and sent long, accusing letters in which she blamed the analyst for all her problems claiming she had felt better before she started analysis. The cutting, splitting, and intense transference neurosis along with extreme dependence on the analyst suggested that Christine might be displaying a borderline personality disorder (see DSM-IV, p. 280), but the depression was foremost at this time.

In spite of the difficulties during analysis, Christine said the depression and pain had abated somewhat. She managed to finish school, met and married her husband, and found a job.

Her behavior became more stable and she functioned rather well, but she never felt self-confident, and she said the "core of pain" was with her always.

The Family Constellation

The Life-Style

> The middle of three, between an older brother and a younger sister, she was born after the death of an older sister. As a replacement child, Christine had a special position among her siblings and she grew up with the belief that she was required to compensate for her dead sister's absence. Her younger sister became a successful rival, more popular and more attractive, but Christine found her place by excelling in academic activities.
>
> Christine accepted her parent's authority and tried to incorporate their values in order to please them. She formed a close relationship with her mother, with whom she could openly display her unhappiness and felt that this entitled her to demand comfort, caring, and service. She was less likely to display her distress to Father, who was more achievement oriented and more likely to make demands.

Early Recollections

> *Four years old*: I was straddling a low fence, playing horsie, and fell and hurt myself in the genital area. I remember lying on a table and Father was holding my hand. A (male) doctor was cleaning me up. I was screaming that it hurt.
>
> *Two years old*: I locked myself in the bathroom. I don't know how. I was standing by the door and Mother and Father were talking to me through the keyhole. They were telling me what to do to open the door. I was so scared I didn't understand, but somehow I got out.
>
> *Four years old*: While I was playing at a girl's house. I fell in love with a stuffed toy dog. I hid it in my sweater and left. I felt guilty, but I wanted it.

Three years old: I was at a birthday party. I was younger than the other girls. I sat on a chair watching the girls play. I felt left out.

Four years old: My parents put me on top of the TV set and said, "You're on TV Isn't that great?" I was scared. I didn't understand. I didn't think it was funny. I smiled a fake smile.

Note that there is a negative mood in all these memories. The person who is depressed will often recall memories that show unhappiness, fear, failure, rejection, and other dysphoric feelings. However, it is also possible that this mood is indicative of a trait as well as a state and such a mood may be part of a dysthymic disorder (see DSM-IV, p. 169) or an axis 11 personality trait cluster with mixed anxiety and depression. Using our rubric for early recollections we find

I am: inept.

Life is: full of pain, fear, and confusion and I don't know how to handle myself.

Therefore: I have to take whatever I can to get even, although I know it's not right.

The early recollections show a lack of social perspicacity. The feeling of inferiority about her social acceptability leads her to act in such a way that the group will exclude her. She doesn't comprehend her parents' little joke. She doesn't really understand other people, and her feelings toward others are negative and angry because she feels unaccepted by others. The world is not a hospitable place for her.

Although her husband loved her, she did not believe she was lovable.

Although her parents loved her, she felt she was a disappointment to them.

She wept. She wept to her mother. She wept to her husband. She wept to her analyst. She wept to me.

She wanted comfort but said she felt like a "burden" to others.

But she never showed this side of herself to friends or colleagues because she wanted to hide her deficiencies from them (as in the TV recollection).

The Therapeutic Relationship

Christine's story demonstrates not only a depression associated with the problems Christine had of perceiving and identifying herself as an unlovable replacement, but also the complications of a transference neurosis with a traumatic loss of the analyst repeating the previous loss of her favored mentor.

Freudian psychoanalysts believe that in order to effect a complete cure, the client must develop a "transference" and work through the transference with the analyst. That is, the client must experience and relate libidinous and hostile feelings originating in early childhood. The analyst becomes the object of the projection and all of the emotions aroused are attributed to the client/analyst relationship rather than to the client/parent relationship. It is this transference that allows the client to re-experience the childhood situation and allows the analyst to understand and interpret what happened in childhood and how it affected the client.

We, however, believe that the creation and working through of the transference may add an unnecessary dimension to psychotherapy since it tends to unnecessarily prolong psychotherapy. Furthermore, the projection onto the therapist of the attributes belonging to figures in the client's past can become a form of resistance to the demands of the present therapeutic situation, which is to uncover and correct mistaken apperceptions. The childhood origin of current problems is usually revealed by an analysis of the life-style. The early recollections are understood as "playback scenes" and we interpret these apperceptions early in the therapy or as soon as the client feels "safe" in the relationship.

After the initial interview, I asked Dorothy Peven to interview Christine to collect the life-style information. Ms. Peven and Christine spent two sessions together and then we met for a life-style review as noted above. I asked Christine to continue with

Ms. Peven on a weekly basis and said I would serve as consultant and see both of them after every third or fourth session. We used the technique of *multiple therapy* often in our office (Dreikurs, Mosak, & Shulman, 1952).

But Christine was still in the throes of a tumultuous, unresolved transference relationship with Dr. K. She was feeling abandoned by her female analyst and that loss made it very difficult for her to trust any therapist (especially a woman therapist). During the information gathering for life-style analysis no apparent problems arose. However, when I asked Chris to see Ms. Peven weekly she was very unhappy and her hostility, anger, and competitive feelings about women (as evidenced by her early history) came pouring out. She did not cooperate with Ms. Peven, questioned her abilities, and accused her of insensitivity and incompetence.*

Some would explain this type of resistance on the part of the client as "negative transference." Adler believed that resistance is part of the tendency of all "neurotic" people to depreciate others. That is:

> I expect from the patient again and again the same attitude which he has shown in accordance with his life-plan toward the persons of his former environment, and still earlier toward his family. At the moment of introduction to the [therapist] and often earlier, the patient has the same feelings toward him as toward important persons in general. It is the depreciation tendency, which underlies the phenomenon Freud described as resistance and erroneously understood as the consequence of the repression of sexual impulses.... [E]very patient will attempt to depreciate the [therapist], to deprive him of his influence.... (Adler, in Ansbacher & Ansbacher, 1956, pp. 336–337)

---

*I later learned that the manner in which Christine related to Ms. Peven was similar to the manner in which she related to Dr. K. She told me that she would scream at the analyst, call her foul names, and accuse her of incompetence and lack of interest.

On the other hand, the depreciation tendency can be considered a cognitive device used whenever one person wants to gain a position of dominance over another or when one feels threatened by a statement or idea that seems to attack one's own perceptions or status. Thus depreciation of the therapist and therapy can also be attributed to the client's fear of domination by the therapist.

We understood Christine's behavior as evidence of her lifestyle tendency to depreciate women and to say she did not understand them since she saw them as excluding her and saw herself as not successful in female-female relationships. In fact, for most of her life Christine's mother was the only woman with whom she felt completely at ease. Ms. Peven and I believed that because of this it was very difficult for Christine to form a therapeutic alliance, a cooperative client/therapist relationship with a female therapist. We decided to take her out of the female-female situation to see if we could get a better response. And so Christine started to see me regularly.

Psychotherapy

While Christine would cry often in our sessions, she never screamed at me or left the room (as she had with Ms. Peven). After all, her hope for cure rested with a man. However, she demonstrated the same kind of accusatory hostility at me as she had at her analyst. I quote from one of her letters to me:

> You know what I think? I think you don't give a shit what happens to me. You don't care one way or the other whether I live or die, whether I'm depressed or not. You just sit there and philosophize for 45 minutes. Then you call me resistant and charge me a lot of money. I don't understand most of what you say, and when I try to tell you that, you say I'm fighting you. You can't stand it when I get really frustrated with the therapy and you don't seem to be very tolerant when I get angry at you. When I feel frustrated and angry at you, you turn it all back on me, blame me, and tell me

it's all my fault, I'm fighting you, I'm resisting, etc.
Maybe you don't like me and you really don't want to
see me, but you're sure willing to take my money. . . . I
don't think you're going to help me, so maybe I should
just give in to it. . . . I'm tired of trying so hard to get
better and not seeing any results. . . . I am so discouraged and pessimistic. . . . What did I do to deserve all
this misery? I must really be bad.

Christine's first sessions with me were filled with the details of
her intense sadness, bitterness, and anger. She was sleeping
poorly and having dreams about Dr. K. and she would wake with
anxiety. She wrote long letters to me describing her painful feelings. She insisted on her own deficient state, could not accept
compliments, and could not accept optimistic predictions. She
was obviously exaggerating her deficiencies, but would become
hostile when it was pointed out to her that in many ways she
was successful in her life.

I began to see that in order to continue with the therapy I
would have to stop all analysis and confrontations and just validate her feelings. It seemed that unless I could accept her as the
deficient creature she kept telling me she was, she could not feel
understood by me. Furthermore, I would seem to be rejecting
her and expecting her to be something other than what she was
and could be.

Thus, I told her I could see how intensely she was suffering
and suggested medication to see if we could reduce the pain. She
could accept this kind of help. I prescribed an antidepressant
and an anxiolytic and for a few months I spent our time together
focusing on symptom response and medication effects. This
allowed us a certain amount of objectivity in our discussions.
For example, she could report frequency of nightmares rather
than dramatically review them. I stopped making any attempts
to reassure her, paid close attention to her complaints, and never
challenged her logic. I would not criticize what she did but only
reflect on it, ask why she chose to do it, and then accept her
answers.

Her symptoms began to improve, either because of medication or the change in my behavior or both. The frequency of nightmares decreased. The crying spells stopped. She began to trust me and to reveal herself. For example, she was now able to talk about her violent sexual fantasies. I listened, but did not contest nor interpret her behavior. She was not ready to stop suffering.

Although the symptoms were decreasing, the therapeutic relationship was still fragile. She wondered if I liked her, cared about her, thought she was smart, good-looking. She behaved as if she had been a neglected child asking for more and more positive stroking. It was highly unlikely that she had been misunderstood or nonnurtured in childhood, but she felt she had been called upon to accomplish more than she was capable of doing and that this had been a "terrible strain." And now she wanted consistent, unfailing, unconditional positive regard, even though she was showing all her flaws.

After a few months spent reflecting feelings and discussing medication, I became able to direct the session contents. I suggested that her suffering was truly her state of experiencing the way she lived in the world. She agreed with this and I was able to introduce the concept of "protest" to her; namely, that her suffering was a way of saying that she was unhappy, that she was "protesting" and wanted the protest heard. Christine was intrigued, but this did not lead to quick change.

Christine continued to air her anger at me, at her job, and at her own inability to change her situation for the better. The hostile behavior was accompanied by accusations against me because she did not feel that she was improving and demanded that I help her more. However, the overall tone of her anger seemed to be decreasing and she was not as consistently hostile as she had been. This ambivalence could be seen in a dream.

I was talking to Dr. K. as if we were two normal people. I was asking her advice about how to get a part-time job. Dr. K. said, "You look younger since you quit therapy." . . . I didn't want her to leave. I wanted to tell

her some of the ways I'm getting better. . . . She said,
"You still owe me $120." I started to cry. I didn't think
I should have to pay her because of all the trouble she
caused me, and then I thought that I would pay her
because I wanted to be her friend.

During our discussion of the dream she could see her own
mixed feelings about Dr. K. and the lessened intensity of the
negative transference (although she was still angry). Then she
had her first dream in which I appeared:

I was with you, Dr. Shulman, and Dr. K came to see me,
to work on something. I was dumbfounded to see her.
Dr. K. said "Hello," but acted as if she didn't know me.
You, Dr. Shulman, were being protective and paternal.

This dream signals a change in her feelings for me. I became
somebody she could see as a protector, somebody she could turn
to (as in the first recollection). This change in attitude helped our
therapy proceed.

Christine complained a lot about her job, and reported
having dysphoric feelings whenever she went into the office. As
was her way, she felt that a great deal was expected of her and
that she was constantly under pressure to perform (always at
the top of her capabilities). Since her self-image depended on
how well she was regarded, she never stopped trying to do
better and better. No matter that she had been promoted and
was entrusted with important responsibilities, it was never
enough. The pressure she put on herself accentuated her fatigue
(she stayed late every night and worked weekends) and poten-
tiated the depression.

I suggested the possibility of working part-time, but Christine
was so committed to proving her worth, of being somebody
"important," she refused to consider reducing her responsibilities at work. She would not give up her ambition.

Yet I knew she was planning to have children and when I
asked her if she was considering pregnancy, she admitted she had
been discussing it with her husband. I ventured that perhaps she

might truly enjoy staying home with a child more than having a career. In the past, when I had suggested that her wanting to start a family was entirely normal, she had accused me of being anti-feminist, a "male chauvinist."* But this time she was able to consider my remarks without getting angry.

This led us into a discussion about values. For example, she had become interested in decorating her apartment with "frilly things." She expressed guilt about this, thinking it was "unseemly" for a modern, intellectual woman to decorate in such a manner. I pointed out to her that she had been talking about a possible pregnancy and the desire to dress up her house seemed to be entirely normal nesting behavior.

The next month she and her husband decided to have a baby, and in a month she was pregnant. Typical of anxiety-prone individuals, she was worried that she would not adequately finish her job responsibilities and that after the birth her relationship to her husband might change for the worse. She also worried that something would go wrong with the pregnancy.

Therapy at this time focused on her anxious anticipation, but there was no doubt that she was also excited. She began to buy layette items and maternity clothes. She stopped taking all the medication and sleeping aids and was now reading the popular journals for expectant parents. She was impressed by one article, which said that men and women were not alike and women had a natural interest in home and children. She reported that she felt better after reading the article and added that previously she had looked down on women who chose marriage and children over a career.

Relapse

Then her mood collapsed again. The anxiety and depression returned. She continued to have what she called "weird thoughts": "It shouldn't be me having this baby." There were crying spells daily, accompanied by thoughts such as "I feel empty. I don't feel whole. I want to feel whole when I have this baby."

---

*Other female clients have said the same.

If she shouldn't be having this baby, who should? Her dead sister? People with anxiety and unclear self-image can have such thoughts. It is as if they doubt their own capacities, identity, and authenticity. Furthermore, they feel they have been dedicated to some particular role in life, whether they wish it or not.

I considered this behavior to be a product of her feeling unauthentic, that is, that all her life she thought she was not free to be whoever she truly was. She thought she was supposed to be something for somebody else and was just beginning to feel authentic when the relapse happened. I hoped to make her see that there was a connection between her negative self-image and the belief that she had to sacrifice herself to relieve her mother's pain, that she was not supposed to follow her own inclinations. Christine accepted this interpretation and we discussed it at length. She said she finally understood what I had been trying to explain to her for lo these many months. With this new insight she was able to see the pregnancy as her most "important business"; not as an aside to her job, but as a fulfillment.

At this time she reported two dreams in one night as follows:

> I had gone to bed with a headache and nausea. [First dream:] I was trying to call my doctor and tell him that I was sick and I saw blood. He wouldn't listen to me and said there was nothing wrong with me. I felt terrible. [Second dream:] I had an appointment with Dr. K. I was late and was trying to call her. I had a piece of paper with old phone numbers on it. A custodian of the building answered the phone and said no one was there. I went to the building where there were a lot of people. I walked to Dr. K's office. I stopped and said to myself, "What am I doing here? I should have called Dr. Shulman." I decided to leave. Dr. K. came out of the office with another person. I shrunk back and felt shy. She saw me and smiled at me. I woke up.

I asked Christine to associate to the manifest content of the dream. She said she believed she was "not being helped" by psychoanalysis and that she now believed that the transference behavior had only reinforced her negative self-image. The dream seemed to be saying: "What am I doing in this place? [This relapse!] I better get out of here. I never was able to get through to Dr. K and it's a mistake to even try. I should have brought the issue to Dr. Shulman."

CHRISTINE: I think the transference is over.
DR. S.: I think we can see the transference as resistance to therapy.
CHRISTINE: Does that mean it was my fault?
DR. S.: No! No! Don't start that negative self-image stuff again. I take it back! Forget what I said!
CHRISTINE: [Laughter] OK I get it.

Recovery

Gradually, Christine began to see examples of how she had not allowed herself to really appreciate herself, follow her own path, and make her own decisions. When Mother tried to give her advice about the pregnancy, Christine resented it. I tried to help her understand that mothers are in the habit of giving advice at these times and she could smile and do what she wanted. Mother would not suffer if Christine did things her own way. Christine had to learn that there was not a one-to-one relationship between her behavior and Mother's feelings. She said she understood and felt free of guilt and "pain" for the first time in her life.

Later, we pursued the early memories in which she experienced rejection. She was now able to distance the feelings of rejection from the understanding of the politics of status-seeking among children. The early memories looked different to her now as she realized that she was not being excluded, *she* was the rejecter. With this comprehension, she was able to start to make friends and enjoy a social life with her husband.

In her eighth month Christine ended therapy. She was enjoying herself and it seemed the pregnancy made her feel that she had proof of her own worth; she had acquired status. She talked about loving feelings for her husband and took a long leave of absence from work and even considered resigning. She began to believe that there wasn't anything more important than what she was doing.

Epilogue

When the baby was five months old Christine came to the office to show him to me and describe her happiness. Three years later I got an announcement of a second child with pictures of both children enclosed. In her note she said, "We are a happy family." She never went back to the office.

—B. Shulman

References

American Psychiatric Association. (1994). *Diagnostic and statistical manual of mental disorders* (4th ed.). Washington, DC: Author.

Ansbacher H. & Ansbacher, R. (Eds.) (1956). *The individual psychology of Alfred Adler*. New York: Basic Books.

Mosak. H., Dreikurs, R., Shulman, B. (1952). Patient-therapist relationship in multiple psychotherapy. In *On purpose: collected papers of Harold H. Mosak* (pp. 36–44). Chicago: Alfred Adler Institute.

8

Icarus

... with melting wax and loosened strings
Sunk hapless Icarus on unfaithful wings;
Headlong he rushed through the affrighted air,
With limbs distorted and disshevelled hair;
His scattered plumage danced upon the wave
—Darwin, in Thomas Bullfinch, *Age of Fable*

He was out of jail for two months when he came to see me. He was very good-looking: tall, with thick dark hair and blue eyes, buffed, with a deep, resonant voice, he wore his Armani suit with élan. He talked easily and practiced a boyish charm, which served him well. In fact, he was perfectly suited for his profession as a divorce lawyer. Unfortunately, he was also a criminal, a man who had drugged his women clients, raped and sodomized them, took pictures of what he was doing and then threatened the women so that they would continue to sleep with him.

He had lost his license to practice law, his wife had divorced him, and his children and former friends wanted nothing to do with him. He was living on the good will of a former client, sleeping on a couch. He was depressed, hadn't slept in weeks, and had lost twenty pounds during his stay in prison. He couldn't concentrate, he believed his memory had been impaired, and he didn't have the energy to look for a job. He was chronically fatigued, had frequent crying spells and waves of sadness. As he cried, he complained that he could not stop going over in his mind what he had done and could not understand what had come over him to make him behave as he had. "I am so sorry. Why did I do it?" he cried. Why indeed?

History

Peter had a troubled history and the story he told was as fascinating as it was appalling. As far back as he could remember he would lie, steal, and cheat.

He recalled sitting at the kitchen table as a young boy pretending to do his homework while he was really reading a book. While in high school he took care of the house of an elderly lady. She was somewhat senile and didn't remember what she owned, so he ransacked her drawers and took whatever he wanted. A straight A student, he won a scholarship to a prestigious law school and was expelled when caught cheating on a test. He finished his degree from a lower-rated school. He was very bright and attractive and made an excellent impression when he interviewed. Hired by a large law firm in Chicago, he soon became their specialist in family law, that is, divorce. His office was in the same building as our office and Peter and I were friendly.

He married Louise while in his mid-twenties and they had two teenage daughters. Over the years of marriage his wife had developed a "drug problem"; in fact, she had become addicted to cocaine. And, while never completely faithful to his wife, Peter had become even more sexually promiscuous in response to a multitude of events which threatened to overwhelm him.

His sister's husband was president of a new biotech company. He convinced Peter that he should invest in the initial public offering (IPO) and advise his partners do likewise. Peter and his brother-in-law were so convincing and Peter was so enthusiastic that his partners did invest (collectively) a very large sum. Peter himself had put all of his retirement accounts into the pool of money. When the company collapsed, Peter had to account for himself. At the same time his wife was hospitalized for detoxification from cocaine, the roof blew off of their house during a windstorm, and his eldest daughter was in trouble in school.

Peter was also involved in an affair with a female colleague and she chose that time to end the relationship.

Peter could not or would not explain what happened next. From a client he apparently obtained the date-rape drug, GHB, put the drug in a cup of coffee, and served it to a female client. He said, "I wanted to see what would happen." When the woman became drowsy and confused he raped her and found it to be the "most exciting sex" he'd ever had. By the time the woman came back to consciousness her clothes were in order. When she asked what had happened, he told her she had fainted.

A few months later, he did it again. Only this time he had a video camera hidden in the bookshelf and taped what he did. Soon, he was sedating, raping, sodomizing, and taping himself several times a week. He also started a new affair with a secretary in his office. After sex with her he would pick up not one, but two prostitutes and take them to a motel.

His wife, Louise, became suspicious of his many long absences from home without adequate explanation. For the first time in their marriage, money was a problem. Arguments and fighting were a daily occurrence and Louise started using drugs again.

One day she went to his office unexpectedly. While waiting for Peter, she came across the hidden camera. Already suspicious and distrusting, she took the tape out of the camera and put it in her purse. She played it when she was home alone and, in a rage, confronted Peter. He told her it was the only time he had been unfaithful to her and swore he would never do it again. Louise was mollified for the moment, but she had hidden the tape and would not give it back to Peter.

About the same time, one of the women Peter had "taken advantage of" experienced pain and discomfort. She went to see a gynecologist who informed her that her genital area had been traumatized. At home, she searched her calendar until she came to the appointment with Peter and remembered that there had been an unexplained lost period of time during her interview. She became suspicious.

Peter was beginning to show changes in his behavior. He was spending money recklessly, calling people all hours of the night and day trying to explain away what had happened to the invested money. He could not sleep and became more and more unreliable at the office. His partners had to take over some of his practice and eventually they asked him to resign.

During this period I met Peter in the hall one day. He stopped me and, in detail, told me what he had been doing and what Louise had found. I was incredulous and asked, "Are you crazy?" He was speaking so fast and loud I'm not sure he heard me and he certainly paid no attention to what I said. He wanted to tell me so many minutiae I excused myself and, as I walked away I thought, "This man couldn't be in his right mind . . . this is not rational behavior."

The next time I saw Peter, he had been asked to leave the law firm, had lost all his money in his brother-in-law's company, and had stopped all sexual activity except for the continuing affair with his former secretary. His wife had filed for divorce, his house was up for sale, and, he said, his wife "was out to get him." He was very concerned about the possibility of charges being filed against him. After an argument, his wife went into a rage and took the tape to a lawyer who suggested that she take it to the Office of the States Attorney.

One month later that which he feared happened: the State's Attorney's office filed charges against Peter. The woman who had complained to her doctor was identified, and she pressed charges of rape. Peter was charged with criminal sexual assault.

He was frightened and thought about leaving the country. He didn't have any money and had to depend on the few of his former clients who still felt kindly toward him to lend him money to pay for his defense. He was living with his girlfriend and he allowed her to take charge of his money. He appealed to everybody he knew and told his "story" over and over again asking for help and money. He went from one lawyer to another until he found somebody who told him if he would plead guilty he would only have to serve two years. Not so. He was tried, found guilty, and sentenced to five to fifteen years in jail.

Life-Style

Family Constellation

Peter was the youngest of four children, born thirteen years after his youngest older sibling and thus a virtual only child. The family had immigrated from the Balkans and Peter was the only member of the family born in the United States. Smart and cute, he was Mother's darling and she doted on him.

His parent's marriage had been "arranged," but, he said, they had learned "to love and respect each other" and "got along well." He described his mother as "an angel" and said she was patient, soft-spoken, easygoing, and sociable. He portrayed his father as "God-fearing and churchgoing" and believed that the children were afraid of him because he was "so strict." The family was devoutly Catholic and Peter served as an altar boy for many years. As a child,

> I had a rapport with Mother and Father that the other kids didn't have. Mother let me get away with things, and I was the favorite of both parents. I was a happy, pretty, smiling baby, and everybody wanted to hold me. Mother overprotected me, but the whole family was proud of me.

Early recollections

> *Four years old:* My brother had a convertible. We drove on a wet, rainy day to pick up my father at work. I was in the car with my older brother and it was raining. I was happy. I was able to go in the car.
> *Five years old:* My oldest brother was in the Navy. I had on his white sailor hat and they put me on the hood of that same car and took pictures of me. It was a nice summer day and I had ice cream. It was warm and nice and I was happy.

These are happy memories where other people admire him and do things for and to him and he enjoys their attention. The recollections tell us how Peter thinks of himself: as a charming, little boy who knows how to be cute and adorable and basks in the attention and admiration of others (although he does nothing to deserve it). And in the following recollection he confirms this.

> *Five years old:* My older brother was at the side of the house. He was cracking coal with a hammer. I was watching him as he worked and he was sweating. I was happy I didn't have to do that.

He is an observer of other people, men in particular, while they do important things, like driving a car and cracking coal. He sees how men behave, but doesn't see himself as doing what grown up men do. He is not active; in fact, he is passive. He is not the instigator of any action; he is the object.

> *Four years old:* A lady told me every child would eat a peck of dirt. So I took a teaspoon and ate some dirt. I didn't think I'd had enough. I thought, "You got to get that peck of dirt in you," so I ate some more. I was trying to be a good boy. I told Mother and she raised hell with me.

In this recollection he believes he is doing the right thing, but shows a lack of judgment. He acts without thinking of the consequences and without collecting appropriate information. He sees himself as naive and he is correct.*

> *Six years old:* It was my first encounter with sex. One girl was thirteen and the other girl was eleven. We were playing in the back yard. The girls cleaned the coal out of the shanty and put down burlap bags. They undressed me and they played with my genitals. When we stopped, the girls told me not to tell my mother. I thought we had a secret. I liked it.

---

*This recollection can also be understood as a warning not to believe everybody. Somebody gave him the wrong information and he believed it.

Five years old: My sister was graduating from high school and the girls' family was baby-sitting me. I was in bed with the two girls and I remember kissing them and hugging them. It was nice.

Eight years old: I rode a bike alone for the first time. It was so exciting, so thrilling, I got an erection. The whole world was open to me.

He is very much aware of sex. In the above three memories he describes how sex is associated in his mind with pleasure and excitement and how he "gets off" on the sensations produced from sex. Also, there is little concern with the right and wrong of issues: events are opportunities. He does not take responsibility for stopping anything.

One way of understanding Peter is to oversimplify his style of life as that of a charming baby. Raised as a child in a world of adults, he was sheltered and overprotected in his early years. The early recollections and the life-style lend themselves to an analysis that suggests that, by playing the psychosocial role of the "baby," he never learned to be responsible or trustworthy. But he did learn how to get along on the basis of his charm.

"Babies" are people who rely on others for nurture and support; they do not take care of others. They expect others to make allowances for them and protect them. They do not live up to a large degree of responsibility and in positions of power may be quite irresponsible.

Peter thought he was invulnerable to the stresses of everyday life. When the charm wore off, that is, when he was faced with the consequences of his misbehavior, he ran from one to another looking for support and nurture. He behaved according to his life-style, that is, as a little boy looking for somebody else to fix life for him.

Analysis

It is tempting to think of Peter as an antisocial personality (see DSM-IV, p. 279). He has a childhood history of lying and stealing, and an adult history of deceitfulness and failure to conform to social norms. Furthermore, he was never guided by the need to be ethical and/or honest. He showed a reckless disregard for his safety as well as the well-being and the rights of others. He acted impulsively, ignoring consequences. I quote from my notes:

> Client does not always use good judgment or evaluate the consequences of his behavior with "common sense" (or logic).

The question of feelings of guilt and remorse appears in most discussions of the sociopathic personality. Peter did not express remorse, nor do I believe he felt guilt. He did express regret, but he never tried to excuse himself to me.

It has been suggested that:

> All of those who fulfill the APD [antisocial personality disorder] criteria may be antisocial, but they may differ greatly in their motivations for being so and significant interpersonal, affective, and psychopathological features such as the capacity for empathy, remorse, guilt, anxiety, or loyalty [influence their behavior]. (Hare, Hart, & Harper, 1991, p. 393)

For many years Peter functioned as a "charming con man" as he *used* others (especially women) for pleasure and profit. He was glib and had superficial charm, but he lied even when it wasn't necessary. He was sexually predatory as soon as he came out of jail and came into contact with women again. It seemed he was sorry he got into trouble, but, in the manner of a child, thought if he said, "I'm sorry," all would be forgiven. He wanted to be taken under a woman's wing where he would feel protected and sheltered and be taken care of, behavior consistent with his life-style.

We look at sociopaths from a particular point of view. In line with our concept of behavior being either socially useful or socially useless, we see the sociopaths' guiding line as living on the "useless" side. On the surface, they seem to behave like members of society, but sociopaths are like sneak thieves; that is, they hide what they are actually doing and get their feelings of superiority from putting something over on others.

On the other hand, much of what Peter did during the period of time he was under stress and misbehaving can be considered manic behavior. He was full of energy and confidence, was sexually promiscuous, needed little sleep, showed impaired judgment, and spent money indiscriminately. He ignored his practice, his wife, and his daughters. He never thought of consequences, he invested money unwisely, and, in every aspect of his life, he was self-destructive. Primarily, he was obsessed with sex* and the sensations it produced. Eventually, it became clear that Peter had suffered from a manic episode that included a profound sexual disorder: bipolar 1 disorder, single manic episode. (DSM-IV p. 173).

When I met Peter in the hall, as mentioned above, and asked him if he was "crazy," I was responding as a concerned friend. When Peter became my client after his years in jail, I realized I had been right to begin with—he had been manic during that period of time.

Characteristic of manics, he made foolish business investments and the strength of his enthusiasm carried other people along with him. His search for excitement and sensation seeking was beyond what any sane-thinking person would consider. It was almost as if he deliberately challenged the gods to see how far he could go. "Manics often put themselves in dangerous situations" (Peven, 1996, p. 81), and surely Peter's behavior with women was nothing if not dangerous, (as well as outrageous).

Peter thought of himself as a "good guy," and there were many very nice traits about him: he was generous, he tried to be helpful, he was kind, and he had good social skills. But he (and his family of orientation) had high expectations for him and he pushed himself to climb higher and higher. Upon reflection, I

---

*Hyperpersexuality is common in the manic phase. What distinguishes Peter's case is that it was the primary symptom.

don't believe he ever really believed in himself or believed in his abilities. He told me that sometimes he was surprised that he had made so much money.

Whenever private goals are inordinate, insatiable, or improbable of attainment, they contribute to psychopathology.

> In the face of high achievement goals, bipolars feel inadequate, and they attempt to compensate for feelings of inferiority by impressing others with grandiose plans.* The plans serve as substitutes for real achievement (Peven, 1996, p. 99)

Why didn't he seduce the women with whom he had sex—as he was demonstrably capable of—rather than drug and rape them? I came to believe that his behavior only made sense when looked at in the light of a manic episode that included sensation seeking.

> Mania can be a denial of fear . . . as well as a denial of sadness. . . . One may attack a challenge when one feels inept or fears defeat, but one can also attack when one smells success. Given the . . . characteristic ways of behaving, it is also quite possible that mania can result from being aroused by a success or by pleasant excitement and not knowing when to stop or moderate the arousal. [Manics] in fact, court the arousal since that is the way they feel most comfortable (Peven & Shulman, 1983, p. 14).

Zuckerman (1979) called the tendency to seek out high levels of excitement the *sensation-seeking motive*. We see this behavior as movement toward the goal of excitement.

> In clinical studies Zuckerman found this motive associated with hypomania, impulsiveness, and overactivity. . . .

---

*Peter's contagious enthusiasm for the plans of his brother-in-law, for example.

[I]t follows that people who use feeling in this way will seek out feeling experiences. . . . [People who are manic] value excitement so much that they intensify these experiences until they provide the amount of emotional arousal with which they feel most comfortable. (Peven & Shulman, 1983, p. 10)

Psychotherapy

I was fond of Peter. He *was* charming and he was kind to me, and he never made any sexual advances. I had sent him a few cards while he was in jail, but we didn't really correspond. So when he came to see me and asked for help in psychotherapy, I was glad to be helpful. But I had a lot to learn about "charming pleasers."

After we had been meeting for a few months, and after learning to understand him better, I realized that Peter had come to talk to me because I was one of the people he came to for help. Peter's method of coping with difficulties was to go to others for help and rescue. In his earliest childhood recollections Peter sees himself not as an initiator of action, but as dependent upon the actions taken by others. In a crisis situation, his modus operandi is to seek help.

At this time in his life, it appeared that Peter was just not able to make a comeback as he had in the past. He seemed to conjure up fantasies about job offers. He hoped to practice law again, but there was no possibility of regaining his license. Yet he pursued ephemeral leads from strangers for positions in the practice of law and he continued to claim that his brother-in-law would make room for him in his new company. I never believed the man would give Peter a job, but Peter seemed to believe every sorry excuse offered. He told me about vague offers from Europe and South America. But no job ever came through. He never collected sufficient information to understand that people were more likely offering him hope rather than a position, never followed up any real opportunities, and resented any inquiries on my part for more information.

Peter told me that he felt called upon to accomplish something special. He was supposed to be *big*, but didn't feel that he was, and apparently was hesitating to test himself to see whether or not he had the goods. Instead, it seemed, he was going through the motions of finding a job while fooling himself into believing that he was making sincere efforts. His (unconscious) plan was to look for a job but not to find one. It is probable he didn't feel capable of holding down a job, but *looking* for a job gave him license to ask for help. He was always "getting ready," and looked as if he were sincere, but when, through friends, I really did find a job opportunity for him, he did not follow through.

He had continued the relationship with his former secretary even though she had appropriated and misused much of whatever was left of his money. While it was apparent to me that the lady had "done him wrong," his naiveté and lack of inquisitiveness won out. He said, "She couldn't help it. She explained it all to me." My notes read:

> He does not incorporate information in a logical way.
> I tell him he is not paranoid enough . . . he trusts certain people without questioning. [As in the fourth recollection.]

Peter was not interested in analysis and did not understand what was required in order to proceed in psychotherapy. He came to see me irregularly and spent his time with me talking about vague plans for a job, his sexual exploits, and the trips he took.

Unfortunately, his defenses prevailed. He didn't actually try to justify himself, he had too much of a sense of social responsibility for that, but, on the other hand, he never expressed remorse. He was sorry he got caught. He was sorry he no longer had the world on a string. He was sorry he didn't have any money. But he never made any logical plans for life after prison. He never pursued a real job offer. He never thought of paying back any of the money his partners had lost. He never paid a penny of child support or alimony. He lived on the good will of a few of his former clients and continued to pursue women who might be won over by his superficial charm. And some women were.

When I suggested the possibility that he had suffered a manic episode Peter was delighted. He now had an explanation for his behavior; he had been "manic." That suited him fine since he decided that it meant he did not have to take responsibility for his behavior. He seemed to be thinking, "I was manic and that's why I did what I did. I was not responsible, 'it' was." He had not come to me to change or learn about himself. He did not want self-examination. It would have been unpleasant and depressing.

People who see themselves as powerless to create and control events are not likely to perceive in what ways they are responsible for outcomes of events. Helping a client of this type to understand and accept responsibility for his or her own actions is a crucial and difficult part of psychotherapy. In those cases where an honest self-appraisal would lead to a severe blow to the self-esteem there is even more resistance to self-examination. Peter could not afford to look at himself.

What is there to be done in psychotherapy when the therapist can't get past the client's defenses? Can I be of help in spite of this? What could I offer?

I believed in him. I believed he wanted to repair his broken life, even if he did not know how to go about it. I thought I could be a support for him while he was turning his life around. Although he had used up his credit with a lot of people, I continued to accept him. I tried to be the "something" he needed—a parent figure, a friend, somebody who validated his being in the world. I wanted to help him to see the world in a less painful way, to deflect his feelings of loss, to find meaning for his life. I tried to bring him *hope*, the feeling that his life would become positive. I wanted him to find meaning for his life and I showed positive regard for him.

Peter taught me that it is possible to be therapeutic without analysis and confrontation. Instead of discussing life-style issues, which he did not want to consider, I spent my time with him using other techniques of psychotherapy: reflecting feelings, clarifying issues, offering advice, and giving emotional support through reassurance and encouragement. And more than once I allowed him to "confess" to me—an old and still useful technique.

*   *   *

Eventually, Peter moved back to his hometown. The last time I heard from him he was living with an "older" woman and she was supporting them both.

—D. Peven

References

American Psychiatric Association. (1994). *Diagnostic and statistical manual of mental disorders*. (4th ed.). Washington, DC: Author.

Hare, R. D., Hart, S. D., & Harper, T. J. (1991). Psychopathy and the DSM-IV criteria for antisocial personality disorder. *Journal of Abnormal Psychology, 100* (3), 391–398.

Peven, D. (1996). Individual psychology and bipolar mood disorder. In Sperry, L. & Carlson, J. (Eds.), *Psychopathology and psychotherapy: From DSM-IV diagnosis to treatment* (2nd ed.). Washington, DC: Accelerated Development.

Peven, D., & Shulman, B. (1983). The psychodynamics of bipolar affective disorder: Some empirical findings and their implications for cognitive therapy. *Individual Psychology, 39*, 2–16.

Zuckerman, M. (1979). *Sensation seeking: Beyond the optimum level of arousal*. Hillsdale, NJ: Lawrence Erlbaum.

9

To the Manner Born

> . . . I am native here
> And to the manner born . . .
>
> —Willam Shakespeare, *Hamlet*: Act 1, Scene 4.

A memory from the age of four:

> I was all dressed up in a frilly red dress, a pretty little girl
> sitting in my bedroom. I think it was my birthday. My room
> was perfect . . . a doll just so, sitting, a book, toys, and
> a little table and chairs . . . like my own little world. I
> was waiting for people to come to my birthday party. I was
> playing in the room all by myself sitting like one of the dolls
> in a chair. Feeling alone with all these *things*. I felt lonely
> . . . waiting."

The Presentation

She was tall and dark and slim. Her name was Marie and she was
twenty-four years old. She sat erect in the chair, well groomed, well
dressed, makeup well done. Her internist had referred her because
she had started having panic attacks about one year before and was
becoming agoraphobic. She told me that during the anxiety attacks
she experienced inner trembling, felt nauseous and dizzy, had
heart palpitations, shortness of breath, and felt a "knot" in her
chest.

She had been married for four years and the problems had begun about two years before when she and her husband, Frank, began trying to have a baby and the doctors discovered she had endometriosis. She had surgery and was put on heavy doses of hormones. She was also taking an antidepressant and medication for anxiety.

At our first meeting Marie reported that in addition to the anxiety, she was feeling depressed, not knowing "where to go" or "what to do" with her life. She said she had had her life planned; she was going to be a nurse, get married, and have babies. But she had quit nursing school in her third year toward a BSN, married, and now would most likely be unable to have children. She said she felt "all at sea," "confused, with no direction." She asked, "Who am I? Where am I going?" and said she "didn't look forward to life." Her plans had not materialized and she was disappointed.

Almost immediately after our first interview Marie was hospitalized for severe abdominal pain and had to have surgery. I saw her often during her stay in the hospital and we had a chance to establish a relationship during which time she told me her story.

The Life-Style

An only child, Marie described her early childhood as one in which she often felt shame and embarrassment. She came from a large family presided over by a grandmother who was the arbiter of family values and who passed judgment on all the family members. There were twenty-four first cousins and she said they were all

> very competitive, but as a child I was ahead of them in all the things they measured when we were younger . . . intelligence, grades, looks. And it turned out that I was the only one that went to college.

Marie thought that Mother and Father were in love with each other and enjoyed their marriage, but she sometimes felt that they were more interested in each other than they were in her. More than once they failed to acknowledge her birthday: "No card, no call, no nothing." Her parents' behavior increased her feelings of loneliness and her feelings of "not mattering" to the important people in her life.

She described her Father as "not much on smarts," a man who was slow, stuttered, and embarrassed her. But she appreciated the fact that he treated her as "Daddy's little girl" and she did "genuinely love" him. On the other hand, she "wanted more from Mother—more attention, more love, more understanding, more loving care." And this was in spite of the fact that Mother was "very protective."

Grandma, who ruled the clan and favored Marie, was quite critical of her daughter, Marie's mother. Marie, who was pampered by Grandma, accepted Grandma's standards. In fact, Marie believed her parents didn't meet *her* standards and she was disappointed that they failed to provide her with better opportunities: neighborhood, culture, money, friends, and so on.

> We lived in a dirty, icky apartment. My Mother was a pig. There were always dirty dishes in the sink, clothes dropped all over the place and scum in the bathroom. I tried to clean up as best I could, but I was always ashamed and so embarrassed about the filthy house, I wouldn't let my friends come home with me . . .
>
> I spent a lot of time at my grandmother's house. I went there every day after school and I loved my grandma, but I resented doing things by myself while other kids' parents took them to skating and swimming.
>
> I was alone. I was lonely. I talked to myself. But I had any material thing I wanted . . . dolls, games, anything.

The Family Constellation

From my notes:

> The one and only, and probably more the focus of the parent's attention than she believed. Somehow, she was born a "lady" and did not approve of the parents' taste,

style, or behavior; they were an embarrassing handicap.

As she was critical of people who did not meet her (and grandmother's) standards, she became socially skilled and looked for her social contacts elsewhere.

As Grandma's favorite, the winner in the Cousins' Sweepstakes, and somewhat "spoiled," Marie thought she was unique and destined for great things.

Early Recollections

Marie's early recollections reflect her feelings of being alone, her sensitivity to humiliation, and the contrast between the way she wanted to be regarded and reality.

The recollection that opens her story (see above) tells us how alone she felt. She knew she was pretty, she realized she had all the "things" she could want, but she felt an emptiness in her life. Her sense of being in the world was about being alone and lonely, almost desolate. She felt "poor in the midst of plenty."

The next recollection is a recurring dream of childhood which we interpret as an early recollection. It is a dream in which she fantasizes about demonstrations of the love she feels is missing.

> I was skiing and I went off a cliff. Then I split and I saw myself falling and also had the sensation of falling. I saw a "poof" down at the bottom. Then I was at the back of a funeral home watching my family up in front crying. I thought it was neat. All my family loved me.*

> *Seven years old:* It was recess at school and there were relay races. A girl tripped me as I was running and I fell flat on my face and skidded on the pavement. I got a big fat lip and a bloody nose. The nuns took me in and made me sit in the class with ice and a rag over my face. I was crying, I

---

*This is the kind of early recollection which an only child will give. Only children sometimes feel deprived of the love and companionship they believe siblings provide for each other.

hurt, but the nuns wouldn't call my grandmother or my mother at work even though I begged them to. I shouldn't have been kept there. Mother was fuming when I told her. She took me to the convent and asked the Mother Superior, "What did she think she was doing? If anything ever happens again, they better get hold" of her. I was embarrassed, but glad.

Eight years old: The nun pulled me out of class into the hall and told me I had B.O. and I smelled. Talk about embarrassed! I felt like a dirty peon. Here I thought I wasn't like my skuzzy house and I thought I was well groomed and she tells me I smell. I was so embarrassed, I wanted to crawl under a rock. I was crying. I thought I did my best to groom myself. I thought a lot of myself.

Five years old: There was a neighborhood grocery store across the street and the lady who ran it was a good friend. One day I went there to pick up groceries. It was crowded and I was standing by the counter. People were talking, not moving. I had to go to the bathroom and I couldn't hold it, so I peed in my pants and started crying. The lady said, "It's OK, go home." I couldn't make a decision; Should I run home without the groceries and face my mother or should I stick it out and wait? Then I lost control. I was treated like a big girl and I acted like a baby. Very embarrassing.

Poor Marie. Although she was trying so hard to be above the dirt and "lower class' culture of her parents, she had not succeeded. Was she afraid that she was a phony and was really just like her parents? This was to be an issue throughout therapy. On the one hand she felt "above all that," but on the other hand, she often questioned herself. Especially noteworthy, however, is the fact that she takes no action even when she feels herself wronged and her failure to act (leave the grocery store in time) leads to decisions being taken out of her hands. In the schoolyard recollection Marie is thrilled to have Mother stand up for her. Her own efforts to get something done, failed—"The nun wouldn't listen to me."

The recollections in which she loses control and the recollection in which she is told she smells devastated Marie, and even talking about it made her cry. She had thought she was acceptable and discovered she wasn't. She was exposed as only a "skuzzy little kid" and not a "lady" after all. Her dream of being "special" wasn't going to come true.

These were, therefore, the issues we would have to deal with in psychotherapy:

1. She felt like a failure when she was not regarded as "special."
2. She exaggerated the importance of avoiding exposure.
3. Her fear of failure/exposure led to hesitation in making decisions.
   a. She delayed decision-making until it was taken out of her hands.
   b. She did not realize that she was sabotaging herself by her own anticipations and expectations.

Psychodynamics

The clinical presentation in this case, anxiety attacks with sensations of trembling, nausea, palpitations, "knots" in the chest, are symptoms of what DSM-IV calls a generalized anxiety disorder (DSM-IV, p. 213). Marie's symptoms began after the discovery that she might not be able to have a child.* The timing of the onset of the anxiety disorder seems crucial. It was a critical point in Marie's life: her "life plan" had fallen through and her whole sense of identity, her self-image, became blurred. In her own words, she was "at sea," "confused with no direction."

Anxiety is a ubiquitous emotion and plays a part in many human behaviors. The psychodynamics of one person's anxiety disorder may be different from that of another's. A fear that something bad is going to happen, a sense of alarm, is charac-

---

*Many young couples in such situations find other ways to have children. Since that didn't happen in this case, I began to wonder if the marriage itself was suspect.

teristic of anxiety, but the function and the purpose of the syndrome of symptoms is unique to each individual.

An important key to understanding Marie's anxiety is to consider the questions she asked, "Who am I? Where am I going?" and her statement, "I don't look forward to life." When Marie presented with these questions and statements, she was saying that her plans had failed and she did not know what to do with her life. Her panic acted as an alarm. She was telling herself that something was *wrong*, that something needed to be done, but she didn't know what. With the realization that she had lost something important, that the "self" had somehow been damaged, the "I don't look forward" statement seemed to foretell the depression that came soon after.

However, anxiety and agoraphobia especially can have many purposes. Anxiety is a feeling as well as an emotion and both are created for a purpose. Anxiety can serve as a catalyst of movement, but it also has a self-protective function, i.e., as an "excuse." The psychodynamics of anxiety often include a goal of avoidance and methods of operation that serve to help the person to avoid the perception and threat of defeat by maintaining distance through fear. Avoidance can become a reward in itself.

We believe anxiety is evoked for the purpose of avoiding "threatening" situations. "Threat" is a label applied to situations that are anticipated to be potentially harmful to the self-esteem. The emotion of anxiety is associated with avoidance behavior. If we do not feel capable of successfully coping with a threat and anticipate failure or disaster, symptoms develop to safeguard the self.

The purpose of Marie's symptoms was becoming more clear. Her dreams were all about "Where am I going in my life? Am I really as good as I think I am? [Do I have B.O. without knowing it?]" She wouldn't go back to school because she was afraid she would become phobic again. She wouldn't try for a good job because she didn't think she could handle anything difficult. Most of all, she feared failure and told me, "I feel inferior when I fail at doing something." And so she did not put herself in the position of really being tested. Her cousins (her cohort) had succeeded and she had not. She was ashamed and humiliated.

Since her health had failed and the onset of the anxiety disorder she had dropped out of the "contest." (One cousin had twin girls that year.) Although she still wanted to impress her family, her symptoms and her tender health kept her out of the race and she could stop competing without losing face; ergo, an anxiety disorder. The perfect "excuse": the "arrangement" of the neurosis. She had lost her place as the winner in the family competition. And then nothing made any difference and she became depressed.

After a few months of therapy she said she was no longer suffering from panic attacks, and no longer experienced "shakiness"; but, she said, "I still feel dull and tired," and added, "I used to feel independent and ready to take on the world, but years of being sick have made me feel vulnerable and tired. I think of myself as a sick person." She felt depressed, lethargic, and worried about herself, and said, "I'm afraid of becoming a weak person, dependent on others, and I hate that."

Marie was disappointed in herself: she had failed to have a baby, failed to get a college degree, her body had failed her, and even her marriage was failing.

She talked about her husband Frank in every session and said she fell in love with him almost immediately upon meeting him and believed she had "moved up" when she married him—he was a "good catch."* But she felt rejected by him since he never initiated sex and often refused her advances toward him. She complained that he would go six weeks or more without initiating intercourse. Sex was a very important issue for Marie and, I believe, Frank made it even more important by rejecting her. The more he rejected her, the more frustrated and angry she became and the more important sex became. She was disappointed and hurt and felt put down by him. "A wife and husband can punish each other by each being unresponsive to the approaches of the other" (Shulman, 1973, p. 89).

---

*The desire to "better" oneself is a time-honored raison d'etre for women to marry.

Why would Frank want to hurt Marie? Was he just not as interested (or as talented) in sex as Marie was and resented her implications and accusations about his "manhood?"

Marie had become sexually active in her early teens and spent the years leading up to her marriage as an enthusiastic sexual partner. Frank intrigued her since he refused intercourse for the first year of their courtship. She truly enjoyed sexual activity and prided herself on her sexual aptitude and felt bitter about Frank's apparent lack of sexual desire. She was obsessed with the thought that he might not want her, especially since it seemed probable she would not conceive.

The anxiety disorder began after the marriage was in trouble. Perhaps she began to realize that she got herself into a bad situation and had made a poor choice. She had married a man who considered himself superior to his "lower class" wife (who wanted to be "upper-class," but secretly didn't believe she was). Perhaps she began to believe that the whole concept of "marrying up" was a fantasy to begin with and that the game wasn't worth the candle. She had been chasing a hollow dream.

Her life-style tells us that in a situation where action is required, Marie does not act. She did not see herself as an initiator of action, so it would not be surprising for her to arrange her life in such a way that others would have to make decisions for her. Therefore, if she did not want to recognize that the marriage was in trouble, what better method of avoidance than the (unconscious) development of an anxiety disorder?

Psychotherapy

When Marie first came to see me, I wanted to help relieve her suffering and so I addressed myself to that task. She was taking medication, but I wanted her to get the feeling that she had some control over her body. One of the methods I use to treat anxiety is to teach my clients relaxation exercises and diaphragmatic deep breathing. I make it clear that the exercises have to be practiced when there are no symptoms present since it is difficult to think about relaxation during an anxiety attack. But, I tell my clients, if they practice when there are no symptoms, eventually they will have some control over the symptoms when the attacks do occur. Those who follow the instructions have found the exercises helpful (as Marie did).*

Marie was reluctant to look for a job and had feelings of conflict about continuing in school. I had been urging her to consider finishing her Bachelor of Science in Nursing. But shortly after the session in which we discussed the possibility of her return to school she experienced a return of the anxiety, and began to be afraid to leave the house. She said, "My big thing is I don't want to fail again."

When she finally started working, she was fired from two (small) sales jobs. Actually, she was too depressed to do well. I encouraged her to believe that she was fired because those "little" jobs weren't worthy of her talents and that she wasn't doing her best because she felt demeaned while working in little "nothing" (her word) stores. She had to start to believe in herself again, and over and over I told her that even if she didn't believe she could do well, I believed it and, for the time being, that would be enough for both of us.

As the symptoms subsided we began to deal with those issues that contributed to Marie's disorder. Marie was a prolific dreamer and so we used her dreams as the takeoff for discussing those issues that most disturbed her.

Dreams

> Had a dream that I had a baby. It had taken me a long time to get one. I was coming home from shopping one day with the baby in the car. I took the bags of groceries into the house and when I came out to get the baby I saw the car going down the street. At first I thought I left the motor on and something malfunctioned and it started to go. Then I realized that someone had probably stolen my car and my baby.

---

*Any success with behavior modification will help to inspire the client with confidence in the therapist so that analytic issues may be approached with some confidence that the therapist has a degree of credibility.

> I was frantic and alone, all alone. I don't know why I
> didn't think at first to call Frank, but I just started
> running for help. I didn't know what to do, but I had to
> do something. I was frantic.

Something had gone wrong. She lost that which she most
wanted and she didn't know what to do. Her behavior became
frenzied, she made no plan for action, and she saw herself as
alone while trying to deal with a catastrophe.

Another dream:

> I got up in the morning and my head was congested; my
> nose and eyes were full and running. I looked in the
> mirror and something was in my nose. There were five
> or six baby mice coming out of my nose. They started
> running around. Then it wouldn't stop; the mice just kept
> coming and coming out of my nose. They wouldn't stop
> coming from my head. [She commented on the dream:]
> My body's infested. My body's infested with rodents and
> it's trying to get rid of them.

Both dreams seemed to pertain to her feelings about her body
and her inability to make babies, to keep babies. All she could
produce inside of her body is sickness and rot. She saw herself
as diseased and full of vermin as if she was saying, "Nothing
good comes out of me."

Dreams such as these will signify and reinforce a depression.
But rather than encourage such dismal thoughts, I attempted to
make an ego-syntonic interpretation. I suggested that her body
was telling her that it was trying to heal itself and get rid of the
putrefaction.

Marie and I spent a good deal of time talking about her feelings about her body. She really enjoyed using her body for sex,
but her lack of ability to reproduce and all the implications
thereof almost succeeded in destroying her sense of herself as a
functioning woman. The lack of sex and the inability to conceive
was destroying her *self* and the marriage.

Even though I knew Marie did not heed warnings, I felt it

was my duty to advise her that her marriage was in serious trouble. It seemed to me she was moving toward a divorce which she may not have wanted. Marie was so indecisive, her intent wasn't clear. And then she brought in the following dream:

> I owned a big house (Victorian style, wrap-around porch). The dream started out with me being at the house and going room to room looking at what the house needed done to renovate it. It had wonderful beauty and charm, but needed a lot of updating. I remember thinking of all the money it would take and if it was worth it. At one point I noted that the floor in the master bedroom was weak, made with thin plywood, and I fell (gently) through to the basement. I came up the stairs and saw a strange woman in the house and she said she needed to talk to me. She wanted to warn me about something in the office. I dismissed what she said as being trivial and when two FBI men came in I started to get angry from all the harassment and started screaming that they should all could get the hell out of my house and leave me alone.
>
> Then the dream went back to centering around the house and what repairs it needed and it became my mother's house and I began to think that I should advise her to sell it and not fix it and spend all that money. She could put it on the market and make 50K without doing a thing and that would be better for my folks.

Whenever a client reports a dream in which he is wandering through a house (and this is a fairly common dream), I assume the client has been thinking about his life and is considering the various areas of his world that are to be examined during the course of therapy. It is a form of self-examination and consideration about what action to take, a way of saying, "This is my life, the house I live in. What room am I in in my life?"

The weakness in the master bedroom suggests a weakness in the marriage. I thought the strange lady in the house was myself (Peven), warning Marie to be cautious. But Marie refused to consider warning signs as important. When she thought of advising her mother to sell, she was considering the end of her marriage. Her life-style was opposed to decisive action so I was aware that she would not act and the therapeutic concern was that she would "pee in her pants' and be forced to a decision not of her own making. Which is, of course, what happened.

With the passage of time Marie began to feel better, the symptoms subsided, and while working at one of the "easy" jobs she was recruited by a big insurance company. With the help of a male mentor, she started to become successful.

There was considerable camaraderie at the office and Marie began going out to drink with the group after work. One night she met an exciting man and started an affair. She was enthralled by the man and his feelings for her and she became more and more indiscreet, scarcely bothering to hide her behavior from Frank. Soon, her drinking became a problem. She became careless and started coming home drunk. After a while, when out drinking with her girlfriends, she would pick up men at the bar and leave with them. She did not try to excuse her behavior to me, she didn't try to explain it either, and, on the whole, she didn't want to discuss it.

Frank became more and more critical and drew even further away. I asked to see Frank and when he came in, his contempt for Marie was evident. He complained about her drinking and "reckless" behavior. He was considering divorce and said the constant quarreling and her late hours were making him angry. He saw himself as "the good guy" and Marie as the "bad girl." Marie could not bear to be thought of in this manner. The woman who thought of herself as "above" felt sullied and dirtied by Frank's accusations, but she also felt justified in her behavior because Frank was so unkind and continued to refuse sex with her. She reminded me of her premarital promiscuous behavior and reiterated how much she wanted and enjoyed sex. John, her lover, gave her love, affection, and *appreciation*.

Eventually, the late nights and drinking became a way of life until one night she went one step too far. She came home drunk and asked Frank to join her and John in bed for a "threesome." That was the end of the marriage. Frank asked for a divorce.

Out of fear that something bad would happen, she tested and tested until it finally did happen and thus confirmed her own anticipation. Since she never saw herself as an active executor, it was no surprise when she arranged her life (unconsciously) in such a way that Frank would be the one to leave the marriage.

Marie had declared psychological bankruptcy. She seemed to believe that it no longer mattered what she did. Although some of her behavior seemed self-destructive, she didn't think so and/or didn't care anymore.

A pattern began to emerge. I realized there had been several occasions when I believed that Marie was heading for trouble and I had tried to warn her, and each time Marie ignored my warning and ended up paying the consequences. I knew she trusted me and was thoroughly involved in the therapy, but that didn't stop her, and it also didn't stop me from discussing the risks associated with promiscuous behavior (safety and protection from STDs). If she was going to continue her drinking and promiscuous behavior, she could at least protect herself.*

Perhaps because we had a strong therapeutic alliance I was never offended if she ignored my advice. Although she disregarded my warnings, I knew she benefited from working with me. I accepted her sexuality, did not depreciate her, showed concern about her safety, and never became an opponent.

I would not and did not discuss the moral issues involved. I understood the sexual aspect of her behavior as her way of dealing with her anger and unhappiness, and, I believed, it would pass (and it did). Marie appreciated my attitude and put up with an occasional "scolding." I believe it made her feel that at least somebody cared about what she was doing and what was happening in her life. Reality or not, she had never had that feeling from her parents. As the memory at the beginning of this chapter shows, she never felt that anybody really cared about her.**

I also made it clear to Marie that I would not confirm her attitude toward herself. She may have felt like "damaged goods," but that was never how I saw her. For me, she was a troubled person trying the only way she knew to move on with her life,

---

*Think *Looking for Mr. Goodbar*.
**One of the functions of therapy is parenting when parenting is required. And very often my interest in my clients can be considered as nurturing.

to adapt, after suffering a great defeat. Her dreams were shattered, she wasn't "special."

I was concerned about her and did what I could to demonstrate this concern and my interest in her. She felt free to talk to me as I didn't reprimand nor would I support her feelings of failure. She was a loving, kind, generous person and a nice human being, and I believed that she could and would find a better meaning for her life. It was important to encourage her to move on.

I thought a great deal about the meaning of the promiscuous behavior since we believe that sex is something a person does deliberately, not just something that happens.

> Why a person uses sex in one way rather than another will be related to his own personal opinion of sex and of life. For example, if he sees life as a competitive striving to get, to have, to achieve, then his sexual behavior will reflect these same propensities and he will have trained himself over the years to use sex for personal triumph in a competitive arena. . . . (Shulman, 1973, p. 8)

Marie said she felt her behavior was justified because Frank had deprived her of sexual satisfaction in her marriage. She was soothing herself. That was possible, but I thought there were other possibilities to be explored. Perhaps Marie felt that it no longer mattered what she did. She could have been making a statement of emancipation: "I'm free to do as I please," a rebellion against any restriction, a declaration of freedom. Possible, but not consistent with her life-style. Perhaps she wanted to demonstrate her prowess, to prove she was attractive, to show her husband that she could get any man she wanted, that men wanted her even if he didn't. I thought the behavior, at that time, was a form of revenge and a way of saying to herself, "Even if my husband doesn't want me, other men do." It became an area of success for her. I believed her behavior was directed against her husband as an expression of desperation. All was already lost. Maybe she just wanted to cut her losses, that is, bring the losing situation to a definite end.

Epilogue

In the last meeting we had after she felt well enough to leave therapy, Marie had recovered from the depression and her grief over the loss of the marriage. She had become a successful insurance agent and had a new boyfriend, Ken. He was divorced three times and had an unfortunate tendency to gamble. Marie tried to reassure me when I expressed apprehension, by telling me he was "well-connected" in certain racing/gambling circles. But I listened with trepidation, and, once more felt obliged to send up the warning flags. With the same result.

Last year Marie sent me a note:

Dear Dorothy;

I'll try to get you up to date regarding men, love, and marriage! Most of the time all I see "flying" are those damn geese, and I guess that could be appropriate with respect to my love life considering what we know they leave behind!!

My folks are aging, and gee, I don't know why, I'm not. Mom has had a few close calls so, as we know from all those years of great therapy, guilt is raging in her Princess. However, because of those years of great therapy I'm trying to resolve all that with as much tolerance, forgiveness, and love as I can before I don't have the chance.

My New Year's Eve will probably involve a lovely bottle of champagne, one pound of shrimp cocktail, and my two cats.

With love and gratitude,
Marie

Still alone.

—D. Peven

References

American Psychiatric Association. (1994). *Diagnostic and statistical manual of mental disorders* (4th ed.). Washington, DC: Author.
Shulman, B. (1967). The uses and abuses of sex. *Journal of Religion and Health*, 6 (4), 317–325.

10

Guilty
Pleasures

No one knows the dark desires of the soul . . .
—Laurel K. Hamilton, *Guilty Pleasures*
(New York: Ace Books, 1993)

The Presentation

Albert came for help when he was twenty-six years old, stating that he had been depressed most of his life. He remembered periods of depression in adolescence, later in college, and since then. The periods were episodic, lasting a few days at the most, but during those times he would feel sad, would spend time in bed, would not feel like working or studying, kept to himself, and felt listless. At those times he felt guilty that he was not accomplishing anything and was ashamed of himself. He said he never entertained suicidal thoughts, but he considered himself lazy and unambitious.

Being a bright young man and socially active in his peer group of college-educated urban friends and fellow workers, Albert had read and heard enough about psychological issues to be aware that his periods of reduced motivation and activity would be considered a depression and that therefore he needed to talk to a "shrink." However, when he was depressed, he had no desire to talk to anyone, and when he was not depressed, he did not think about it.

Although the depressions had continued periodically for many years, he had come for help at this time because he felt the depression was interfering with his ability to work. His boss had begun to notice and made remarks about Albert's absences and slowness in completing his assigned projects. Albert realized that he might lose his job and, what would be worse, acquire a reputation for being an undesirable employee. He didn't want the depression to affect his whole career.

A good-looking man, Albert was well dressed, well groomed, and well spoken. But on that first day he seemed to be to be in great distress and said,

> I don't know what's happening to me. I don't know what
> I'm doing. Please help me. I need to get over having these
> "time-outs." Some mornings I want to get up and go to
> work. I look forward to it—other times, I resent getting
> up. I don't want to go to work. I don't tell anyone how
> I feel. I don't even want anyone to know that this
> happens to me.

A review of his symptoms revealed little else. He had no problems with sleep. When not depressed, he could stay up late and enjoy the company of his friends and still rise on time for work in the morning. When depressed, he often sought the company of friends who made him feel better, but said he was more irritable and less friendly. Having social acumen, he understood that irritable behavior was not seen as favorable in his peer group. He tried to remain tactful, kept a smile on his face and excused himself, leaving the group earlier rather than later. However, his main complaint was his loss of interest in and motivation for his work.

Current Life Situation

Albert worked for an advertising agency as a graphic artist. He considered himself a good artist, competent in his field, and he already had a reputation as an "artist to watch." He was proud of the fact that some of the agency's clients were so pleased with his work that they asked for him specifically. Albert even thought of himself as being better than the art director, his boss. But he was tactful enough to keep this opinion to himself. Although he deliberately made friends with the clients to win their favor and keep them asking for his services, he was astute enough to know that the art director might not be happy about his becoming too much of a favorite.

He enjoyed his social life, had friends of both sexes, many of them former schoolmates. He had no committed relations with women, but had enough money to have his own apartment and to enjoy his friends and peers. In fact, being with them often brought him out of a sad state, while being alone increased his sadness.

He felt close to his parents who lived nearby and spoke to them frequently. He had dinner at their house at least once a week and spent all holidays and family occasions with them.

History

Albert was the only child of European immigrants who came to America in the late thirties as refugees from political oppression. The family members included aunts, uncles, and cousins and there were strong family bonds. The family was comfortable, but not wealthy. Father worked as a manager in a restaurant that other family members owned, and sometimes Mother helped out.

Albert had been a bright child who was dearly loved. He had shown an early talent for drawing and was encouraged by his parents. He also had been a headstrong child, often arguing with his mother before making peace with her. He considered his mother to be "anxious" and "timid" and sometimes felt restricted by her.

His father was a passive man, quiet, involved in his work, usually doing what Mother wanted him to do. Since Father was passive, Albert found him less intrusive than mother, but also less available. He said Father was polite, quiet, and "probably depressed." He recalled many times that father would sit quietly and not participate in conversations.

Albert had an early memory, from age seven. He was with his parents. Father was sitting on the sofa, looking unhappy. Mother was sitting at the table, crying. It seems inspectors wanted to close the restaurant and Mother was afraid Father was going to lose his job. Albert said,

> I wasn't sure what it meant, but I knew somebody was doing something bad to father. I felt puzzled and sad. I was mad that some inspector could hurt my Father. But I was scared, too, because I didn't know what it really meant.

Although Albert did reasonably well at school, he didn't like it. He enjoyed learning, enjoyed being thought of as bright, but found sitting in a classroom boring. He sometimes made mischief in class by talking to classmates or clowning around. He never got into serious trouble because he seemed to know how far he could push the situation and was careful not to be openly defiant.

He was best at, and enjoyed most, being creative. He excelled in subjects like art and history, but was also quick in arithmetic and physics. He had a memory of winning a spelling bee at the age of six:

> The teacher told me I had won because I spelled "cricket" right. I felt very proud and I wanted the other kids to know. I liked the teacher.

In college he majored in the arts and did very well with creative projects. He decided to work as an illustrator and graphic artist because he felt he was more likely to make a living in graphic art and, he said, he "had no desire to be poor and struggling for recognition" in the fine arts. He graduated from a local academy with honors and easily found jobs. People liked his work and this reinforced his creative attempts.

Albert spoke a lot about his job and his ambition to start his own studio and freelance. He seemed very practical in discussing the risks, but also seemed determined to try. When he was most depressed, he would tell himself that if only he could get his own business under way, he would be more motivated to work. I suggested that some of his behavior might be a passive-aggressive resistance/defiance to his supervisor and he readily agreed. He began to make serious plans to leave his job, saved enough from his salary to begin his own studio and discovered that his so-called laziness had greatly decreased. He was more active, more outgoing, and more productive in his work than he had ever been. He depression had lifted and he wanted to take a vacation from therapy.

Psychotherapy with Albert had been relatively simple. He had a specific complaint related to his occupation and did not seem to experience any impairment in any other aspect of his life. He did not suffer any disabling symptoms and the dialogue in psychotherapy was mainly about his relationship to the art director and his disinclination and his procrastination doing his work. Consequently, that is what we discussed.

I would ask questions or make comments directed toward clarifying and specifying his perceptions of situations, his emotional responses to the situation, and what he intended to do. I would frequently ask, "What do you plan to do?" "What is it you really want?" I ask questions such as these in order to help clients clarify for themselves their own direction of movement. And I ask clients to predict what the outcome will be. ("How do you see this ending up?")

Albert did not bring into the discussion any areas of his life that may have been embarrassing to him. He had no reason to raise any defenses and he didn't. He enjoyed our meetings and the work that we did in identifying the nature of his problem and the possible solutions. He was pleased to be learning about and talking about himself. The therapeutic relationship was easy to establish, easy to maintain. There was a therapeutic alliance and he easily achieved his goal.

Dynamic Formulation

Albert was a one and only child, admired by his parents, talented enough to win praise and socially adept. He measured himself against his father and decided that he wanted to be more powerful and successful. He could hold his own in his relationship to Mother because he depreciated her demands by thinking of her as being too timid. He did not suffer from low self-esteem; he felt secure in his competence. Even as a child, he could take a stand and resist being "bossed around" by others. His resistance could be open defiance or more covert mischief and the fact that he never got into trouble showed political acumen and pragmatism in his interactions.

His early memories show both the positive and negative sides of life. To be weak and at the mercy of others is frightening and abhorrent. To be competent and achieve public recognition is desirable and rewarding. His ambition was to be good enough so that others would recognize his talents and grant him status, and to be his own master so that he need not depend on others. In his own words, he wanted to be recognized as a "major art figure in the advertising world."

I did not see Albert for several months. From time to time he sent me a copy of some of his work, which looked good to me. He was chosen to illustrate a book and advertising companies were beginning to contract with him for special projects. He felt successful, productive, enjoying his work. And he had developed a relationship with a young woman and was thinking about marriage.

He returned to see me in November, about a year later, because he had become depressed again. He could not understand why. He had gradually begun to feel tired of his work, spent less time at it, was less motivated, felt less creative, and became alarmed at the way he was feeling.

Given Albert's original history of having felt depressed most of his life, I had to consider the possibility that Albert suffered from a recurrent mood disorder, perhaps an inherited tendency to mood swings. I had to wonder if Albert's period of successful productivity could be an upward swing in a mood cycle. At the same time, my understanding of Albert's early development suggested to me that he had grown up in a family atmosphere that contained sad and timid people. And that being sad could have been a learned behavior, what Alfred Adler called "self-training" in a role to play in life (Adler, 1918).

I took the opportunity to ask Albert about this new depression, its symptoms, its timing, its effect on his sleep and dreams, and what were actually the thoughts in his mind. Albert said he felt pressured by his obligation to arrange a family get-together for Christmas. Apparently, his parents had relied upon him to make all the arrangements for the past several years. He called the aunts and uncles and invited them, arranged for the food and catering service, and acted as the friendly host. He enjoyed it the first few times, but he found himself wanting to spend more time with his friends than with his parents and relatives and felt guilty and ashamed that he was so selfish.

He had the same "symptoms' (engaged in the same behavior) as he had in the past. He began to sleep later in the morning, to be less productive in his work, to avoid returning telephone calls, and to feel bad about himself.

Psychotherapy

This situation gave me the opportunity to interpret to Albert the meaning of his behavior. I pointed out to Albert that the more he talked about Christmas, the more depressed he seemed to get. I asked him if he was becoming depressed because he really didn't want to have this burden, or, was he feeling burdened by the obligation because he was depressed?

> DR. S: Would you be happy to host Christmas if you were not depressed? Is this something you really want to do? Or is this something you feel obliged to do?
>
> ALBERT: I really don't want to do it. [He thought for a while longer and said:] I feel like I should do it. I don't have a good reason for saying no. I would be ashamed to look so selfish.
>
> DR. S: Then, if you are going to do it anyway, even though you'd rather not, are you going to feel sad and unhappy about it?
>
> ALBERT: Are you telling me I can stop the way I feel? Are you telling me I can control this depression?
>
> DR. S: Well, perhaps; sometimes, depression actually is a kind of whining.

About a month later, Albert returned from a trip to a convention and reported that when he got to the convention he did not immediately see anyone he knew. He described how he stood in the lobby and watched other people gathering in groups and greeting each other. He began to feel lonely and sad. The he caught himself and told himself, "I don't have to get depressed about this: I can't gain anything by getting depressed. I came here to have a good time and that's what I'm going to do."

He reported that as soon as he made this decision, he immediately stopped feeling sad. He began introducing himself to everyone who wore a convention badge and returned from the meeting with the feeling that he had had a good time and said he understood much better what I meant when I told him his depression was kind of hidden resistance to doing the tasks he was facing; it was a way of dragging his feet and making a silent protest against the demands of his life.

He then found a way to solve the holiday party situation. After Thanksgiving dinner he announced that he expected to be out of town at Christmas and New Year's and expressed his regrets that he would not be able to host the next party. He was pleased that this actually caused little problem since other family members were willing to take on the job.

From that point on, Albert reported a marked decrease in frequency and intensity of the depressive episodes: "I don't know if I could do this if something really sad happened, but it's hard for me to stay depressed. I seem to start laughing at myself when I start to feel sad."

By now, Albert had started his own studio and was doing well. He came for therapy sessions at infrequent intervals. He was able to face challenges directly, to ask himself what he wanted to do. He could be decisive, yet dutiful. His relationship to his parents became easier for him because he recognized that they were actually more anxious than they had to be and that he did not have to limit himself because of their anxiety. He felt less guilty when he saw them worrying needlessly.

After a few more months he felt free of depression and stopped therapy, but he stayed in contact and would continue to send examples of his work.

Two Years Later

Several years later, Albert returned with a new problem. By this time, he was married and the father of one child. He was successful in his work and not experiencing depressive episodes. His presenting complaint was that he was overeating. Specifically, he was eating candy. He especially liked chocolate bars. He would keep a supply of bars and eat them in his car after work when he was on his way home. He confessed that his wife and office personnel did not know he was doing this and no one had remarked that he was gaining weight, but he had gained ten pounds and did not like it. He was eating three to five candy bars a day and he was ashamed of his behavior because he considered it a weakness. He described how he never brought the candy into the house or office. He would eat in private and carefully dispose of the wrappers.

"Why am I doing this?" he asked.

The appearance of a single symptom or behavior that begins to occupy a part of the person's life space suggests that the behavior is a sideshow, a displacement of a conflict from one area to another. In a healthy young married man, the underlying conflict would probably be found either in his occupation or his marriage. Albert claimed that he was happy and felt creative in his work. The most logical place for me to look was in his marriage.

Albert was quite willing to discuss his marriage. His wife, four years younger than Albert, was the youngest daughter of a family with the same sociocultural background. She was bright, well educated, worked as a schoolteacher, and she and Albert seemed to get along well. Albert took the leadership in their social activities, as she was less outgoing and was happy to have him make their social plans. He had a few complaints about her housekeeping, but decided this was not important enough to fuss about.

Actually, all had gone well until the birth of their daughter. As joyful as he was about the child, he also felt the weight of the obligation to be good father.* His wife seemed happy being at

---

*The responsibility of being a new father rests heavily on the shoulders of some men, who experience anxiety as a consequence.

home with the infant, but depended on Albert to be helpful to her
when he came home. A carefree social life was now less possible,
since the infant's requirements took priority. The obligation eventually seemed to have a negative effect upon Albert. He noticed
that his wife was less attentive to him and lavished love upon the
child. Albert was too mature to compete with his daughter, but
was not willing to give up the previous admiration he had received
from his wife. He thought she had become less interested in sex
and added that idea to the mental file in which he had stored his
opinion of her housekeeping.

This is what probably opened the way to a covert protest
against the situation. But he was no longer "lazy Albert" having
trouble getting up in the morning. Nor was he willing to dampen
his creativity; he enjoyed his artistic and commercial success.

During this period he became mildly interested in a young
woman working in his office. She was attractive, appealing, and
definitely seemed to like Albert. He met her after work several
times and thought about starting a relationship. Whether he
actually did or not is not clear to me, but Albert stated that he
did not. He concluded it would only complicate his life and affect
his career. So, in his words, he "put it out of [his] mind."

Analysis

What Albert *did* do was to become a secret chocolate eater. This
may have been less exciting than secret sex, but it was a lot less
complicated for a person who approached life in a pragmatic
way. By making it secret, by labeling it as "naughty" behavior,
by planning when and where he could buy, hide, and eat the
chocolates, the rather simple act of eating could be elevated to
the status of a sinful act and thereby become more pleasurable.
It took us just a few sessions to sort this out. We both agreed
that this was a more pleasant symptom than being depressed.

I thought about why it was important for Albert to keep his
eating behavior secret. Simply overeating would have had no
"resistance" attached to it. Even eating chocolate bars is to imply
a weakness, not a vice. But eating chocolate bars *secretly* has the
smell of a covert rebellion against something. Although he

intended to fulfill all his marital and parental obligations, he still objected to some of the limitations imposed on him. By keeping it secret, eating chocolate was not only a private enjoyment, but also a self-gratification. His position was that he would do his duty, but he would also take care of his own desire for rewards and even out the balance between the sacrifices and the rewards.

The flaw in this plan was the undesired weight gain. Weight gain for Albert was a sign of sloppiness and incompetence. It was this undesired after-effect that had brought Albert back to see me.

Albert felt guilty about the secret eating, but was not yet ready to give up the chocolate. Ever creative, he joined Overeaters Anonymous and participated in a 12-step program. He soon became the leader of his group. Of course, this took him away at times from his wife and child, but he was always with them at least some part of every day, except when he was out of town. And, after all, it was for a good, helpful cause.

Now, reducing his chocolate eating became a goal. But the secret rebellion had been turned into a public behavior that was socially acceptable. The time he put in at Overeaters Anonymous put a limit on his feeling of dutifully being present to care for his wife, honor his parents, and parent his child, because he now had something important—another obligation—that could be used to keep himself at a distance from the demands of the family. He had arranged to have a worthwhile cause to explain why he could not always be available. I accepted that at this time in his life Albert could not tolerate more intimacy and stronger commitment and so he had arranged a neat way of doing what he wanted and looking good at the same time.

Summary and Conclusions

It was easy to work with Albert. His goals were clear to him and he caught on quickly. I allowed him to take the lead in presenting issues in our sessions since he knew what he wanted to achieve. Since he was well aware of his ability to become resistant when he was dissatisfied with a situation, he was able to visualize his depression as a passive rebellion. Furthermore, his depression itself was a rather mild form of dysthymia with no serious vegetative symptoms (see DSM-IV, p. 169).

Albert was actually a likeable young man who behaved in responsible ways. He was ethical in his business and social relationships and caring toward friends and family. He wanted to do the right thing, wanted acceptance and admiration. He could be charming and was successful in his chosen work.

But obligations and duties can sometimes become oppressive and one looks for "vacations," "excuses," or "outs." Guilt feelings are common if one fails to do one's duty, and without the necessary respites duty can become oppressive. Most of us learn to find a balance between duty and "time off." Our own human limitations must also be recognized; we can strive for perfection, but must accept that we are imperfect. Albert's own ambition and demands upon himself came face to face with his own intention—not to be mastered by anyone or enslaved to any situation that forced him into an unwilling behavior. Thus Albert could visualize his obligations as holding him down—a situation he wanted to avoid. He was creative enough to balance duty and freedom from duty in such a way that he was responsible, yet free.

I have touched briefly on the question of diagnosis. On reflection I do not believe Albert had a clinical depression, and perhaps it would be a mistake to even call it depression. He was given no medications. He became sad when he found himself in a situation that demanded that he do things he really did not want to do. He became unhappy when he didn't like the situation. As soon as he freed himself from the situation (decided to start his own studio) or realized that he was choosing to suffer rather than change his behavior (as at the convention), he would stop feeling sad.

There were no great stresses in Albert's life nor were there destructive personality traits. Perhaps the best way to understand Albert's "depression" is to view it as a learned behavior, modeled by his father, as a passive, covert way of "dragging his feet" when life asked more than he was willing to give.

—B. Shulman

References

Adler, A. (1959). *Practice and theory of individual psychology*. Paterson, NJ: Littlefield, Adams. (Original work published 1918).

American Psychiatric Association. (1994). *Diagnostic and statistical manual of mental disorders* (4th ed.). Washington, DC: Author.

Epilogue

Our book is about our theoretical perspective, which is based on a biopsychosocial model (Dilts, 2001), and how it is used to help people who are challenged by life's events. We approached the telling of each story in a hermeneutic fashion, interpretive and explanatory. We met the clients, we observed, we asked questions, formed opinions (diagnoses), and proceeded with the dialogue. For each client we designed a unique approach; that is, we fit our "method to the madness" and tried to arrange the therapeutic experience according to what we thought was required.

Should we use behavior modification, interpretation, reflection of feeling, or be more generous with support and encouragement? The reader may wonder at the patience of Dr. Shulman, the playfulness of Ms. Peven, but we believe we have demonstrated that not all therapists need use the same methods (nor probably even the same theoretical model) in order to succeed since experience informs that the success of therapy is more largely dependent on the will of the client to change than it is on the skill of the therapist.

What had we, together with the client, actually accomplished? We believe we had achieved a change in perceptions—about the self, about others, about one's place in society, about what is important and what is not important, about recognizing what each situation calls for, about how one sabotages oneself, about limits and boundaries, about the difference between the possible and the impossible.

For example, Sheri learned to get on with her life and to stop making a "career" out of the incest. Albert turned a vice into a virtue—he managed to feel well-intentioned while he avoided what he considered onerous obligations. Mike learned to feel more benign toward others once he realized others were not thinking unkindly about him. His life became easier as he learned to behave in a more friendly fashion. Even George was beginning to turn himself around when the accident happened. As for Peter, a person's need for help is sometimes greater than his need for self-knowledge. People in great pain cannot deal with introspection.

What do we want our clients to understand from psychotherapy? We want our clients to respect themselves, to recognize their worth, and thereby become able to recognize the worth of others. We want them to be better able to handle stress, to accept the responsibility for their behavior, and to learn not to take themselves too seriously. We want them to understand that how one behaves in a relationship determines the relationship. We would like our clients to resist temptation and to recognize danger ahead (*viz*. Marie). We would like them to become mature adults who take care of themselves; i.e., fulfill their obligations to themselves and others. We want our clients to formulate a redefinition of their situation and start the journey toward self-actualization; that is, to develop their abilities, talents, and humanitarian instincts. Hopefully, they will have tools they didn't have before our rendezvous, for we suspect there are changes that take place that we do not know nor do we understand.

The game of life is a non-zero-sum game: everybody can win. We are the facilitators.

References

Dilts, S. L., Jr. (2001). *Models of the mind: A framework for biopsychosocial psychiatry*. Philadelphia: Brunner-Routledge.

Index